Black Street Speech

BLACK STREET SPEECH

Its History, Structure, and Survival   by John Baugh

 University of Texas Press, Austin

Requests for permission to reproduce material from this work should be sent to Permissions, University of Texas Press, Box 7819, Austin, Texas 78712.

LIBRARY OF CONGRESS CATALOGING IN PUBLICATION DATA
Baugh, John, 1949–
  Black street speech.
  (Texas linguistics series)
  Bibliography: p.
  Includes index.
  1. Black English.   2. English language—United States—Social aspects.   3. English language—United States—Spoken English. 4. Afro-Americans—Social conditions.   5. Afro-Americans—Education—Language arts.   I. Title.
  II. Series.
PE3102.N42B38   1983   427'.973   83-10578
ISBN 0-292-70743-6
ISBN 0-292-70745-2 (pbk.)

To my grandparents,
Ginnie, Minnie, Curley, Bob, and John

Contents

Preface

One of my first childhood memories was of my mother changing her speech during telephone conversations. As I grew older, it became fairly easy to tell if Mom was talking to someone black or someone white, based on her speech alone. This experience was reinforced by others, and it has always triggered my curiosity: how can people speak the same language, but with so many different dialects? Television was just beginning to make a major impact on society when I was a young boy in the 1950s, and the combined exposure to mass media and black street speech only served to heighten my interest. This book represents a culmination of those childhood observations.

My parents, who both hold doctorates, were very concerned about education, and they stressed its importance constantly. As everyone knows, language skills are a critical component of successful education. My parents were careful to correct my grammar, even when I didn't understand the reasons for their suggested changes. Throughout my public education and my college training, teachers and professors reacted negatively to street speech, yet my personal experiences with friends and relatives contradicted the belief that speakers of vernacular black dialects were inherently stupid or ignorant.

At a young age I was in no position to grapple with the intricate linguistic issues associated with this topic, but as I grew older and became exposed to a wide variety of ethnic dialects in Los Angeles, my fascination with dialect differences continued to grow. As happened to many black students in the public schools, very few of my teachers offered me genuine encouragement. In fact, one of my high school counselors suggested that I study auto mechanics, since I showed some interest in car repair. Anyone who has had their car repaired recently might not consider my counselor's suggestion to be bad economic advice; however, this nonacademic encouragement was misplaced. My math aptitude was high, so I entered a community college to study accounting. I didn't mind accounting too much, but I had several elitist professors that I just couldn't tolerate.

During my brief encounter with the college of business, I was required to take a course in public speaking. I did fairly well in the course, but other black and hispanic students did not fare so well. It was at this stage of my college education that I decided to study street speech more thoroughly.

I changed my undergraduate major to study communication and rhetoric, and one of the first articles that I read on street speech was Labov's classic "The Logic of Nonstandard English." At the suggestion of some of my professors I contacted Labov, who invited me to his office and home to discuss my interests in greater detail. More than anyone else, William Labov has been most responsible for directing my research interests on this topic. Others, including Dell Hymes, John Fought, Erving Goffman, William Bright, Walt Wolfram, and Ralph Fasold, provided additional help and insights along the way. My preliminary concerns were quite narrow; I was concerned only about an adequate description of black street speech, and the balance of linguistic science was of very little interest to me when I first began this work. However, with the advantage of time and training, my research now looks at the language barriers that face other oppressed populations around the world.

During the 1970s, when I developed this work in earnest, I had no idea what my future research would be like, but I knew it would be necessary to develop a methodology where as many blacks as possible were consulted. Several young linguists, particularly young black linguists, provided me with helpful suggestions at every stage of the analysis. I am grateful to John Rickford, Mary Hope Lee, Bobbie Smith, Arthur Spears, Greg Guy, Anne Bower, Don Hindle, Mark Baltin, and Marilyn Merritt, among others. Their ideas and feedback helped refine my approach through the years of fieldwork and analysis.

On a more personal level, I had the advantage of strong support from my family and friends as well. Robert Radford, Sarah Fought, Holly Carver, and Frances Terry have all provided vital technical assistance, and I could not have completed this project without their help and patience. Additional support was provided in part by grants from the American Council of Learned Societies, the National Science Foundation, the Ford Foundation, and the University of Texas Research Institute. Ultimately I am most indebted to the black consultants from across the nation who allowed me to record extensive interviews. They tolerated awkward situations and often made allowances for my innocent mistakes. Through the years I became friends with several consultants, and these gradual friendships were not only a major asset to the research but provided me with rich personal experiences that I will always cherish.

I
Introduction: Street Speech as a Social Dialect

Everywhere in the world, people are sensitive to language, especially to their local dialect. All of us know when we are in the presence of strangers, of anyone who is foreign to our native customs. It is largely for this reason that we tend to judge people, often harshly, by their linguistic skills or by their lack thereof. Our concepts of eloquence may therefore vary greatly, depending on our cultural point of reference. When people share linguistic and social norms, we think of them as comprising a homogeneous group. The specification of group boundaries is nevertheless a complicated task., I have consequently chosen to examine one small slice of black American culture, namely, the common dialect of the black street culture. My remarks are not limited to my personal experience or to fleeting visits to the ghetto: I have conducted over two hundred hours of tape-recorded interviews with black Americans across the United States.

Although there can be no question that significant numbers of black Americans still speak some of the most nonstandard dialects of English found in the world today, it would be erroneous to associate the language of black street culture with all black Americans. The men and women who provided me with gifts of their time and conversation have only one thing in common: they are members of the same race. Their social backgrounds, education, regional history, and shades of skin span the broadest spectrum.

My years of recording in Los Angeles, Philadelphia, Chicago, and Texas have taught me that many people are emotionally involved with the topic of black American dialects. Some people argue that a nonstandard dialect is essential to cultural identity, while others see vernacular black speech as an impediment to success. A few even argue for both positions at the same time—as being complementary. In this context black Americans are no different from any other Americans who disagree about a common issue. In order to examine black American dialects with the clearest possible focus, let us first consider certain historical parallels to another nonstandard

English dialect. Cockney has been spoken by the lower working classes in London for centuries. The upper classes in England, on the other hand, speak a standard dialect known as received pronunciation. Through the years Cockney has survived in the face of sporadic abandonment and various social pressures, but the dialect endures as a testament to the cohesion and survival of the Cockney speech community. One need only look to the linguistic dilemma in *Pygmalion* to appreciate the different social forces that operate on the way we speak:

> HIGGINS [*in despairing wrath outside*] What the devil have I done with my slippers? [*He appears at the door*].
>
> LIZA [*snatching up the slippers, and hurling them at him one after the other with all her force*] There are your slippers. And there. Take your slippers; and may you never have a day's luck with them!
>
> HIGGINS [*astounded*] What on earth—! [*He comes to her*]. Whats the matter? Get up. [*He pulls her up*]. Anything wrong?
>
> LIZA [*breathless*] Nothing wrong—with you. I've won your bet for you, havn't I? Thats enough for you. *I* dont matter, I suppose.
>
> HIGGINS. You won my bet! You! Presumptuous insect! *I* won it. What did you throw those slippers at me for?
>
> LIZA. Because I wanted to smash your face. I'd like to kill you, you selfish brute. Why didn't you leave me where you picked me out of—in the gutter? You thank God it's all over, and that now you can throw me back again there, do you?
>
> HIGGINS [*looking at her in cool wonder*] The creature is nervous, after all.
>
> LIZA [*gives a suffocated scream of fury, and instinctively darts her nails at his face*]!!
>
> HIGGINS [*catching her wrists*] Ah! would you? Claws in, you cat. How dare you show your temper to me? Sit down and be quiet. [*He throws her roughly into the easy-chair*].
>
> LIZA [*crushed by superior strength and weight*] Whats to become of me? Whats to become of me?

Liza clearly placed a lot of importance on learning the standard received pronunciation, at least initially. Most readers are familiar with the scene where she offers to pay Higgins for his service, but she did so as an adult—an adult with strong social aspirations. She felt that mastery of the language could pave the way to greater personal success. In doing so, however, she eventually realized that her new linguistic skills would be unacceptable to those who valued Cockney in the community where she was raised.

Many black Americans face a similar linguistic paradox: although they grow up surrounded by peers who value the nonstandard dialect, when they enter a professional society another style of speaking is demanded. Without drawing too many analogies to Cockney, let us say that isolation from the standard dialect and, perhaps, active resistance to acquiring the dialect of the social elites may help explain the survival of black street speech. Just as some native speakers of Cockney have learned received pronunciation, many blacks have mastered standard English. Such people are a minority within a minority, and they usually revert to their first (that is, nonstandard) dialect when the appropriate situation arises. The practical problems of using "improper" speech occur when a speaker needs to know how to speak "properly." Minorities, by virtue of being minorities, have been isolated from the social environments where the "majority" dialect thrives. It is largely due to this plethora of social, psychological, historical, and linguistic reasons that educators have encountered so much difficulty teaching minority children in the public schools.

Again, because of the emotionally evocative nature of this topic, my decision to concentrate on analyzing speech is based, in large measure, on scientific grounds. Linguistics has occasionally been referred to as the physics of social science, because spoken utterances can be recorded and analyzed as physical commodities. This physical measurement can in turn be controlled under laboratory conditions with high levels of accuracy. This is not to suggest that linguists have solved all their theoretical problems; we can, nevertheless, trace the speech patterns of people who share the same languages and dialects, and through this analysis we can begin to understand more about each group. Because language is a by-product of human evolution, the dominance and use of languages in our modern time tell us a great deal about ourselves and our history. Thus, while I acknowledge the direct influence of social, political, and other forces on black Americans as a group, I have chosen to study language because it represents one of the more tangible keys to understanding the social dynamics of any people.

To switch analogies, time-lapse photography represented a major advancement in the study of movement and erosion. Similarly, the tape recorder gives us a time-lapse perspective on speech that our spontaneous senses cannot detect. Many of my recordings have been conducted with the same individuals over a period of years in a variety of social circumstances. I also obtained permission to conduct the recordings from each consultant. Thus, by comparing the speech of the same individuals on different occasions, I began to see systematic alternations. These linguistic adjustments were made to meet specific conversational and functional needs. In much the same way that still photography cannot capture movement, isolated observations about black speech or the occasional overheard sentence will not provide adequate evidence to examine dialect style shifts. The tape recorder is therefore a vital instrument in my analysis; over the years people have come to expect to see me with my recorder in hand. It was only through such a long-term procedure that I was able to record continuous conversations, thereby capturing dialect adjustments as circumstances changed.

Linguists have introduced a variety of new terms to account for black American dialects, but most of these terms have been rejected or criticized for one reason or another. My research on the subject illustrates a volatile linguistic picture, where a series of speaking styles is common to different black Americans. This fact should not be surprising since all speakers, regardless of language, have their personal range of formal to informal styles of talking. The reason that this phenomenon is more complicated for black Americans has to do with the breadth of speaking styles that are actively used. Speakers with different backgrounds will possess ranges of styles that reflect their personal history and social aspirations. It should therefore come as little surprise that most blacks who speak standard English also hold professional jobs or are the children of professionals. There are, of course, the noteworthy exceptions, yet they are few when compared to the general pattern. I therefore like to think of black American dialects as dynamic entities which, as does the chameleon, adapt to blend in with the immediate setting. This position contrasts with the image of the "Black English" community described by J. L. Dillard:

> If Black English is not identical to Southern white dialects—although it has influenced the latter over a period of two centuries or more—there remains the problem of who speaks it. The best evidence we have at the present time—and it is admittedly incomplete—indicates that approximately eighty percent of the Black population of the United States speaks Black English. (*Black population*, in this case, would mean all those who consider themselves to be members of the "Black" or "Negro" community.) (1972:229)

Dillard's observations set the stage for understanding black street speech, and we are now in a better position to specify the styles of speaking that are used by the 80 percent whom he refers to. There can be no question that a majority of black Americans share some aspects of what is commonly thought of as street speech, although different aspects may appear with different frequency for various speakers. This is the natural result of the social diffusion of black America. In much the same way that Professor Higgins and Eliza Doolittle tried to replace her Cockney dialect, black Americans have gradually come to make systematic and measurable adjustments in their speech to fit more formal situations. However, racial boundaries in the United States complicate the *Pygmalion* analogy, because black Americans will still stand out in a predominantly white group, even if they have mastered standard English.

The mass media has demonstrated that blacks are quite capable of mastering standard English: it is often difficult to identify the ethnicity of announcers without the corresponding video support. As mentioned, these individuals are nevertheless a minority within a minority; the dialects that are used by highly educated black Americans would provide material for another book. My analysis is based on the speech of blacks who have had limited contact with whites. It would be wrong to imply that all my consultants are uneducated; rather, their training needs to be viewed within their own ethnographic context. For example, some of the more "successful" blacks whom I have interviewed, say, those who have completed college and now hold professional positions, are likely to be heavily in debt with mortgages and car payments. Several other consultants, although they did not have a college education, owned their homes, and their used cars were purchased with cash. Because of cultural differences, where street speech reinforces group boundaries with every intercultural exchange, many whites at first glance would consider these people to be destitute.

American blacks have long been aware of dialect differences within the racial group; in fact, such folk terms as "city rap," "country talk," and "talking proper" distinguish different types of black speech. My research was concentrated in urban areas. Most of the data were collected in Los Angeles, but I have gathered additional data in Philadelphia, Chicago, Austin, and Houston. It is largely for ethnographic reasons that I have adopted the term "black street speech," because it conveys a similar meaning to most of the black consultants whom I have interviewed, regardless of their social or regional background. Street speech is the nonstandard dialect that thrives within the black street culture, and it is constantly fluctuating, as new terminology flows in and out of colloquial vogue. I would therefore suggest that we need to think of street speech as a flexible dialect; this is not a conservative standard dialect where archaic forms are preserved by prescriptive tradition. Street speech survives because there is a population of speakers who use it in their daily lives and know that it is the appropriate style of speaking for their personal needs.

In the past I have characterized black street speech on linguistic and interactional grounds, because the nature of the dialect is fluid. The styles of speech that are used on the street may, or may not, be used at home or on the job, depending on the corresponding linguistic values or demands.

The social networks of street consultants have served my purpose, because we can trace the parameters of the speakers' linguistic worlds, and through their contacts we can come to know the special pressures that different cultural values place on their speech (compare Milroy 1980). My consultants are clearly at a disadvantage in a white society that views street speech as an ignorant dialect. The social distance between the groups has been sufficient to drive perceptual wedges between blacks and whites. As a consequence of this linguistic dilemma, many street speakers remain silent when standard English is the dominant dialect. The perceptions of "appropriate speech" and "dominant dialect" are relative to the social realities of different individuals. My research reinforces a fact that seems almost too obvious to mention—namely, people tend to adopt styles of speaking that are suited to their social needs and personal aspirations. In a white-dominated society that has traditionally tried to relegate blacks to the lowest social stratum, access to standard English has always been a tremendous battle.

It is also important for blacks to appreciate why many whites are insensitive to their linguistic plight and heritage. When a child begins to speak, the first language is learned with the greatest ease. In fact, it is the miracle of child language acquisition that represents the keystone of modern linguistic theory. The problem of insensitivity to black street speech is clouded because standard English speakers naturally find their own dialect easier to speak. And, because of the negative values that are associated with street speech, there is very little motivation for whites to learn nonstandard black speech. Whites most typically imitate black speech when they mock minority accents, which are often part of racist jokes and therefore restricted to limited social contexts. Also, street speakers become particularly sensitive when whites try to adopt black speech patterns; this is usually viewed as patronizing because the whites are perceived as talking down to the blacks. Therefore, what is natural to the standard English speaker, because it was acquired with the ease of any first language, translates into a much more complicated situation for street speakers, who face the more difficult problem of trying to acquire a second dialect.

The issue at hand is consequently not one of genetic or intellectual inferiority, resulting in linguistic deprivation; it is more properly a reflection of the difference between acquiring a first language versus the more difficult task of acquiring a second dialect of the first language. The standard English speaker in America is not usually required, at least on social grounds, to learn another dialect of English. Similar problems are faced by some whites who speak ethnic or regional dialects that are judged negatively outside of their group and/or area (for example, Appalachian Mountain speech). They too have witnessed the difficulty of mastering a second dialect, and many of these people reflect their loyalty to their group by maintaining the dialects of their ancestors. For blacks as a whole, the question of dialect loyalty has been cast against a backdrop of poverty and other isolating cultural factors. For many the first steps out of the ghetto came in the form of adopting the norms of more successful Americans. The negative attitudes toward black speech are largely responsible for the stylistic variation that thrives in all black American communities, but it would be wrong to suggest that most street speakers exhibit identical styles. All the consultants whom I have interviewed adopt more standardized speech while simultaneously eliminating aspects of street speech in very formal circumstances (for example, court appearances or conferences with teachers at public schools), albeit with varying degrees of proficiency. It is this chameleon quality that is the primary object of my work.

Linguistic behavior is a vivid indicator of black survival for several reasons. Sociological insights can be gained from the (dis)use of street speech, and educators will be better equipped to implement successful pedagogical policies for students who bring street speech to the classroom as their native dialect. This practical utility can be realized only when we appreciate two fundamental differences between standard dialects and their nonstandard counterparts.

Haugen (1972) described the contrast in the following way. A standard dialect is characterized by a minimum amount of linguistic variation. Nonstandard dialects of the same language exhibit a greater range of linguistic variation. From a social perspective, however, the utility of these styles is inverted. The standard dialect can be used with the broadest social scope and acceptability, whereas the

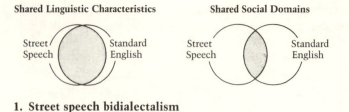

Shared Linguistic Characteristics   Shared Social Domains

Street / Standard   Street   Standard
Speech   English   Speech   English

1. Street speech bidialectalism

nonstandard dialects are acceptable only in a limited number of circumstances. This important contrast is illustrated in figure 1.

Like Cockney, street speech survives in the face both of active opposition and of the increasing numbers of blacks who need to adopt standard English as part of their professional training. At this point the question of linguistic schizophrenia would seem to be logical; after all, if there are pressures for group loyalty and pressures to stop using street speech, how does the individual cope with this constant tug-of-war? This is actually less of a problem than might be expected, because the various dialects seldom overlap in the same speaking context. Thus, when I went with one of my consultants to a court hearing, his linguistic behavior was formal; when we returned to his house and recounted the ordeal to his wife and brotherin-law, he used black street speech. Again, the issue here is not so much the fact that speakers possess formal and informal styles— everyone has experienced this phenomenon—rather, street speech covers a greater range of linguistic styles, which is why it persists as a boundary for social demarcation.

If street speakers face a dilemma, it is one not so much of being torn between two forces but of learning how to move from one extreme to the other with ease and proficiency. Most of the early educational programs to help blacks learn standard English began with the objective of eliminating street speech; this was seen as a dialect that should not be tolerated. This practice reinforced the negative impression of black speech that was already held by the dominant culture. Sensitivity to the special problems surrounding the acquisition of a second dialect was not built into these early programs. In fact, the general practice was to try to teach standard English to blacks using foreign-language techniques, which often resulted in more confusion than clarification for street speakers.

On a global scale, then, we find that street speech is much like many other socially stigmatized dialects, which thrive in societies where other "prestigious" dialects are spoken by highly educated people. In Northern Ireland, England, France, Belgium, and Germany, for example, there are strong attitudes associated with various regional and social dialects. In some of these countries, critical social consequences are linked with these stereotypes. Yet, in much the same manner that Vulgar Latin came to influence changes in Classical Latin, the life of a dialect and language is dictated by the population that preserves it through use. Indeed, the birth and spread of languages have historically reflected the changing trends of human domination. Just as some species have become extinct with the encroachment of both natural and synthetic disasters, so too have some languages become extinct as the numbers of their speakers dwindled. While social attitudes play a major role in the life of languages and their dialects, political domination still remains one of the strongest motivational forces affecting language. In most cases the nonstandard dialects are seen as inferior to their standardized counterparts, but this, again, will depend on the vantage point of the observer. Without question, we find that speakers of nonstandard dialects have been relegated to marginal positions in their societies. As observed, their dialects have minimal social utility, especially in the face of strong negative opinions.

This minimal social utility has a direct impact on individuals. During the years that I have studied this topic, I have talked to black college students who felt an urgent need to acquire standard English so that they would be treated as equals in their classes. Others have expressed the frustration of knowing that they were qualified for advanced positions, only to be rejected because they didn't speak "properly." It is on this personal level that the tragedy of dialect insensitivity takes its greatest toll. The difficulty of acquiring a second dialect cannot be underestimated here, especially for those who wait until they are young adults. For example, certain wealthy families in Texas send their children for speech lessons at an early age to help them get rid of their twang. A great deal of time and money has been invested for this purpose. Most average black college students, on the other hand, may have used street speech with their peers before entering college, thereby delaying the point in their lives where they began to make an active effort to learn standard English. We now find many black children who are learning standard English as their native dialect, but these are the children of blacks who have frequent access to nonblacks, and often these black children have very limited—if any—contact with their poorer street culture counterparts.

Because of the numerous stereotypes about blacks, which tend to be exaggerated in the media, most nonblacks assume that blacks who speak standard English have overcome tremendous personal barriers; but, like so many second- and third-generation immigrants from Europe, some blacks have acquired standard English as their native dialect. We are therefore faced with a complex situation where a variety of personal decisions can directly influence the dialects that are learned and used by blacks in America.

Opinions on "bad" English abound, but there is comparatively little in the way of hard linguistic evidence to support early pronouncements on the subject. The taped interviews that I have collected represent the documentation for my observation that street speech is comprised of several flexible styles of speaking. One of the main reasons why my orientation differs from that of other researchers results from the unique practice of repeatedly interviewing the same adults under different social circumstances. Most of the early studies examine isolated black youths on a single occasion; with the newer advantage of long-term study, the true nature of vernacular street styles is exposed with greater clarity (see chapter 3).

Regardless of how we feel about minority dialects and the negative values that are so often associated with them, they are part of the cultural fabric of our society, and it is in this context that children come to adopt the personal values which they will carry into adult life. Like those who have studied this subject before me, I recognize that historical evidence can clarify the nature of contemporary speech, and this historical evidence may, in turn, be beneficial to street speakers. It is largely for this reason that I have chosen to focus on the language of the black street culture, because this is the dialect that thrives among urban blacks who have minimal linguistic contact with those outside their community.

2

The Birth of Black Street Speech

At first glance the birth of black street speech seems to be a fairly straightforward topic, where historical records would be examined to reconstruct the early stages of dialect development. But several factors, including strong prejudices among scholars, have restricted the scope of these studies, to say nothing of their quality. And, once the questions of racial difference and inequality are added, the topic becomes even more complex. The best historical studies of street speech have been completed during this century, as interest in the general topic of black studies has matured.

Understanding the question of racial equality-inferiority is essential to a full appreciation of the early investigations, because much of the historical research was designed to address this question directly. With the proper historical insights, social scientists and educators presumed that they would be in a better position to know why modern street speakers did so poorly in school. In recent times the debate has focused on two opposed positions: street speech was considered to be either *different* or *deficient* when compared to standard English. Depending on how this question is answered, the contemporary consequences for street speakers could be severe. The sociopolitical climate at different points throughout American history has greatly influenced the objectivity of our early social science.

It will therefore be useful to maintain a distinction between the research on the history of street speech and its *actual* history, because different opinions are common. Four noteworthy trends have evolved over the years regarding the development of street speech, and, depending on where one stands, these may be seen as either helpful or detrimental. The earliest writings, going back to the birth of the nation, were, quite simply, racist. Advocates of white supremacy would point to "Negro speech" as definitive evidence of the intellectual inferiority of blacks. The first serious scholarship was produced by American dialectologists, who stressed the English foundations of street speech. The dialectologist position has been challenged more recently by students of creole languages, who looked primarily at African languages and slave trade jargons as the basis of street speech. The creolist hypothesis is still very popular among many scholars and laypersons, because it provides supportive evidence that reinforces black pride and nationalism; moreover, the creole position emphatically views black speech as being different from standard English—not inferior. The creolists were subsequently among the first legitimate scholars to establish strong links between American blacks and the African continent. However, in the fertile climate of popular support, a balanced historical picture did not emerge until very recently. The most current historical studies suggest a combined hypothesis, where aspects of the creole and dialectology positions interact to create street speech; this seems to be quite logical, since Africa and England have both left linguistic impressions on Afro-American English throughout the Americas.

Because all black Americans ultimately have their roots in Africa, where oral linguistic traditions prevailed, modern historians face a special problem due to sparse—and often questionable—data. Unlike the conservative standardized languages in Europe, where centuries of written traditions influence educated speakers, oral languages tend to change to suit the needs of each living generation of speakers. Those who are familiar with English writing and colloquial speech know that we no longer pronounce the /k/ in *knight* or the /b/ in *climb*, but we accept these archaic spellings to preserve the conventions. The dilemma facing the linguist who is interested in street speech is somewhat more cumbersome, because the "standard" for nonstandard speech is shaped through day-to-day conversations—and not by teachers or grammarians.

I will be concentrating on how these historical analyses reflect on the debate about black intelligence. And, more important, I will focus on why this unique linguistic past has given rise to *flexible* styles, where speakers tend to adapt their speech patterns to suit each situation.

To start at the beginning, then, when slaves first came to America they were considered to be property by nearly everyone. The abolitionists debated this point, but the humane dimension of the topic was quashed by the more pressing need for cheap—and reliable—labor. As beasts of burden the slaves were relegated to positions of inferiority, and racial differences made it easy to perpetuate the gap between black and white societies.

The only voices of moderation that could be heard during this early period of slavery were white voices. Slaves had no rights; it was even illegal to teach them to read and write. During this time the racist literature flowed like a swollen stream. Few voices cried out to protest the rising tide of racist opinion, as the human tragedy of slavery thrived. Contacts between blacks and whites differed in the North and South. In the North very few whites had extended exposure to blacks, that is, in a broad range of social circumstances. The southern experience, by contrast, was very different. Slave overseers, who were among the lowest social class of whites, as well as wealthy plantation owners, who had house slaves and "mammies" for their children, lived and worked in close proximity to black people. In spite of these regional differences, both areas practiced racial discrimination in one form or another. The racism that lingers today has been born from the stereotypes and prejudices that were imposed—although centuries ago—to keep the races apart.

Unfortunately, one does not have to go too far back in American history to find accounts of these distorted and self-serving opinions. The following quote is just such a painful reminder:

> Collectively, the untutored Negro mind is confiding and single-hearted, naturally kind and hospitable. *Both sexes are easily ruled*, and appreciate what is good under the guidance of common justice and prudence. Yet where so much that honors human nature remains—in apathy the typical wooly-haired races have never invented a reasoned theological system, discovered an alphabet, framed a grammatical language, nor made the least step in science or art. They have never comprehended what they have learned, or retained a civilization taught them by contact with more refined nations as soon as that contact had ceased. They have at no time formed great political states, nor commenced a self-evolving civilization. (Campbell 1851:172)

The entire statement is wrong—emphatically so from a linguistic point of view.

To concentrate, once again, on the true history of street speech, one major distinction logically accounts for the dialect differences that falsely supported the assumptions that blacks were inherently inferior to whites. Black slaves coming to this new world were systematically isolated from other speakers of their native language. Slave traders engaged in this practice, thereby deliberately planning the death of African languages, to restrict possible uprisings during the Atlantic crossing. As we shall see in greater detail later, most white immigrants—although poor—were able to keep the language of their homeland until their children and grandchildren learned English as their native language. Slaves, on the other hand, did not have the advantage—and the communicative luxury—of being able to use their mother tongue. This linguistic isolation is unique to American blacks: with the possible exception of Hawaiian natives, no other American minority has faced this type of linguistic isolation through involuntary capture.

Minstrel shows and the early portrayals of blacks in films and on the radio tended to give popular credence to racist scholarship, passing myths and stereotypes from one generation to the next. At this point in history, however, we have made sufficient strides to dismiss this biased literature as an embarrassment to American scholarship. White American racists were not the first to engage in self-serving ethnocentric writing—the foundations of British anthropology, for example, have long been criticized for similar false notions of supremacy—but America needed slaves to help build the nation, resulting in ethnocentricity in our own backyard.

The racist literature about blacks and black speech in particular should, of course, be dismissed in any serious analysis of the subject, but we must appreciate that the opinions expressed by white supremacists—while often absurd—reflected the feelings of a majority of white Americans. This resulted in a social climate, after the Civil War and beyond the turn of the century, where more liberal thinkers tried to present "Negroes" in a better light. Frederick Douglass did much to retard blatant racism among intellectuals, but American dialectologists were among the very first linguists to treat blacks as equal to other Americans. In fact, the dialectologists contended that it was unfair to analyze the speech of black Americans differently from that of other groups (compare Williamson and Burke 1976).

Upon close reflection, we now know that the dialectologists overstated their case, but it would be wrong to suggest that these oversights were motivated by racism. In fact, the opposite really holds true. In the social climate of America from the 1920s to the 1940s, when the dialectologist position was prevalent, there were pervasive racist attitudes toward anything that was associated with Africa. The portrayal of blacks in films from this period has been analyzed extensively by movie critics, who have observed that false impressions—while historically inaccurate, for example, the Tarzan films—nevertheless influenced the real impressions of the average American viewer.

It was against this rigid backdrop of negative opinion that dialectologists began to raise their voices, claiming that "American Negroes" were not exotic primitives but Americans like any other immigrants. In turn they argued that efforts to view "Negroes" as a special (that is, inferior) group would only accentuate public opinion that the races were in fact unequal. The noteworthy exceptions to emerge during this period can be found in the writings of Melville Herskovits and in the work of his student Lorenzo Turner, who wrote *Africanisms in the Gullah Dialect*.[1] These writers were viewed quite skeptically when their work first appeared; but with the eventual rise of black nationalism, from the 1960s through the present time, the stature and popularity of their work have grown.

In the 1980s it is all too easy to criticize the efforts of the dialectologists, who are still quite active, because they failed to stress the African side of the issue. But this is an unfair criticism when the historical and sociological climate is taken into account. From the 1920s through the 1940s dialectologists represented the voices of moderation, and they—nearly alone—maintained the position that black Americans were linguistically equal to their white counterparts. I am compelled to stress this point, because the polemic that saturates most recent writings on this subject tends to be extremely harsh on the dialectologist practice of looking primarily at English influences.

To recap the main thrust of their position, then, dialect differences between whites and blacks were examined in much the same manner as other regional dialects. This practice assured that no group would be treated differently from any other. Nevertheless, this procedure alone proved to be inadequate as far as the history of black street speech is concerned.

By contrast, the creolist hypothesis emerged with primary emphasis on African languages, and this position is still strongly advocated by several scholars who study black American dialects. In order to fully appreciate the nature of this research, however, we need first to look at some of the factions within the linguistic profession itself.

The most advanced linguistic research focuses on analyses of educated dialects of the "classic" Romance and Germanic languages, extending to other language families with strong written traditions. The historical reconstruction of each of these languages, say, of those that grew out of Latin, is a precise enterprise, where evidence from centuries of written documentation is carefully pieced together. These reconstructions provide historical depth to the contemporary studies, where the most common practice leads modern

1. Turner was strongly influenced by Herskovits and Kurath, who developed American dialect atlases.

linguists—as native speakers of their own (educated) dialects—to create their own data based on personal intuitions. Because other scholars typically speak, or are extremely familiar with, these well-documented languages, the intuitions of one scholar can be checked by the informed intuitions of another.

However, there can be no question that the practice of using oneself as a source of "scientific" evidence will have severe restrictions, once analysts encounter a language and/or dialects for which there is little or no existing documentation. In short, this is the very situation that faced analysts of black speech in the United States, and it is still a major factor affecting the quality of historical research on black street speech. Whereas most European immigrants came to America from a homeland with a strong written tradition, African slaves were taken from a land where elders memorized oral histories (see Alex Haley's *Roots*).

For my purpose here, analyzing (educated) dialects—with their long-standing prescriptive traditions and their inevitable retention of archaic forms—differs considerably from reconstructing the indigenous oral languages of Africa. With this distinction in mind, we are in a much better position to view the role of creole studies within linguistics as a general field of study. First, to clarify the relevance of this distinction, some basic terminology needs to be defined.

When slave traders first went to Africa, they obviously did not know how to speak the native African languages. In much the same way that Pilgrims tried to communicate with native Americans, new contact languages were born. Such contact languages—called pidgins—are not native to their speakers. The pidgin results from the need to communicate with people who do not speak your same language. And a pidgin represents the emergence of a new language, which is specifically born out of the contact of two—or perhaps more—other languages. In social terms pidgins tend to be stigmatized, trapped under a shroud of social domination. They usually hold a deferential position compared to the language of those who control political power, which is typically a source of influential linguistic contact.

Once speakers of the pidgin have children, and these children learn the pidgin as their native language, a transformation takes place: the pidgin becomes a creole. In other words, a creole is a nativized pidgin that can usually be distinguished from the original parent languages on several linguistic grounds, including grammatical, lexical, and phonological distinctions, among others (compare Hall 1966). This is why creoles are so easy to detect in the Caribbean islands or in any other place where new languages are born from the collision of two or more other languages.

For obvious historical reasons, the documentation regarding the birth and growth of creole languages does not compare, even modestly, with the excellent documents that have been used in the reconstruction of Indo-European languages. And it is largely for this reason that creolist scholars were not taken too seriously by linguists who were working with more "classic" languages. This was especially true when linguistics was trying to become an autonomous social science in the early 1920s. Such a situation was, of course, very troublesome to creolists, who felt—with ample justification—that their work was being neglected.

There can be no question that the isolation of creolist scholars among other linguists influenced the nature of their research. In much the same manner that the social sciences have tried to imitate the rigors of physical science methodology, however falsely, creolist scholars attempted to imitate the successful efforts of their colleagues in "classic" historical linguistics. Creolist scholars likewise came to spend tremendous amounts of time locating obscure documents from the slave trade; in the case of street speech, many of these documents were records of people who were directly involved with the capture, transportation, and sale of slaves.

Some disturbing problems arise from this situation, because far too many creolists tried to make strong historical statements based on highly questionable evidence. In fact, it is not uncommon to find historical discussions of street speech that selectively cite documents that concur with preconceived hypotheses, while contradictory evidence of equal (poor) quality is dismissed (see Dillard 1972). This problem is beginning to subside because creole studies have advanced greatly over the past two decades, and the work of several scholars has substantially improved the overall quality of research on contact languages. But the traces of the early biased research tradition have left strong impressions on contemporary analyses of street speech, and, as I have indicated previously, the creolists hypothesis received its strongest support in the popular (black) milieu, because of the African foundations of the position. In fact, Dillard wrote the following statement about "Black English" and its history:

> Undoubtedly, the proponents of the East Anglian origins theory and of purely geographic variation (except for the complications of "archaism") have not realized that in their account of the Negro as an archaizing speaker the picture which emerges

is that of a racial archaism—a Negro who just can't catch up or keep up. This is surely the most blatantly racist position which could be presented, if all of its implications are intentional. Since similar linguistic forms occur in the West Indies, on some parts of the West Coast of Africa, and even in Afrikaans, only the kind of historical explanation which scholars like Whinnom, Thompson, Stewart, and Valkoff give could possibly provide a basis for linguistic dignity for the Negro. The idea is so new—and terms like pidgin are subject to such general misunderstanding—that even Black leaders are sometimes resentful of what may seem like a less favorable presentation of Negro language history but one which, upon close examination, turns out to be the only one consistent with Black self-respect. (1972:10–11)

It is my personal contention, as a scholar and a black man, that black self-respect will be enhanced by the truth—even though it is riddled with painful reminders of the social consequences of racism, poverty, and exploitation. Biased scholarship, no matter how it masquerades as a psychological panacea, will only continue to provide a partial image. The history of street speech is not a unilateral issue, either from Anglican or from African sources. I do not mean to imply by this that neither position is correct; rather, the best historical evidence shows that a combined hypothesis is the most accurate, at least at this time.

In order to illustrate this point, we can look at a single example of a street speech dialect feature and review the corresponding assumptions that intersect with the various historical positions. The example that I would like to consider is the use of *is* in street speech or, more specifically, the three variables involved in sentences like "He is coming" > "He's coming" > "He coming," which are all used in street speech.

As American dialects continue to merge through the gradual erosion of once rigid class, regional, and racial barriers, the dialect differences that remain provide—in a very real sense—a half-life cycle as important to linguists as carbon dating is to archaeologists. The rate of subcultural osmosis (that is, the mainstreaming of American subcultures) can be measured by the distribution of dialect differences. For reasons that are still obvious, black Americans have not overcome these barriers with the speed and ease of white immigrants. The racial barriers are less important to my observations than is a full appreciation of the corresponding influence on the development of black and white dialects.

Is, almost more than any other linguistic characteristic, has been examined in great detail to determine the absence of the verb *to be* in black street speech. It would be wrong to imply that street speech does not use *is*; rather, it is used very differently in standard English. Labov (1969) observed that street speech could omit *is* in the same linguistic environments where standard English uses contractions. The typical speaker of the black street vernacular uses all three possibilities and therefore produces a complex pattern of alternation that is influenced by linguistic and social forces alike. There has been a tendency for dialectologists and creolists to disagree on the use of *is*. As might be expected, both positions are plausible, but both start from completely different points of departure; the main difference lies in the direction of historical change assumed for black street speech. Do speakers have *is* as an underlying aspect of their dialect, or does the vernacular have a vacuous (that is, Ø) form that gradually gives way to the intrusion of *is* as speakers gain more exposure to standard English? I am, of course, simplifying the issue tremendously for the sake of illustration. The historical oppositions are as follows:

Dialectologists   is > 's > Ø
Creolists   Ø > 's > is

As we shall see momentarily, both positions hold some validity, and it is the combination of hypotheses that reveals the most feasible explanation to date. This debate among linguists, which is far too technical for the discussion at hand, is secondary to the fact that nonstandard black speech can be distinguished from all white dialects of American English based on *is* usage alone (compare Wolfram 1974). It is largely for this reason that such a small word has received so much scholarly attention. Yet, in spite of the good intentions of every linguist who has ever worked on this topic, significant distortions of the facts abound in popular books on the subject. For example, at first glance the following comic strip, which has been used in linguistic texts to illustrate black English, suggests that Mary Frances is omitting *is* from her speech:

LUTHER   **BY BRUMSIC BRANDON, JR.**

© 1972 by the *Los Angeles Times*. Reprinted with permission.

A similar example quoted to illustrate black English appears in Dillard's major work on the subject:

> The standard example is
> (1) My brother sick . . .
> The child who said
> (7) My brother's sick
> probably was indulging in some kind of code-switching under the influence of Standard English. *Proof* [emphasis my own] of this is that he also says
> (11) They's sick
> (12) I's sick . . .

Dillard then goes on to illustrate another example of code switching which, as we will see, is pronounced quite similar to number 1 above and therefore is undetectable in speech:

> (18) My brother be's sick [for a long time]
> where (18) carried over the basically meaningless (in Black English) 's of *They's sick, He's sick*, etc. (1972 : 52, 54)

My observation is a simple one: these examples are different in print only.

Recalling that these examples have been drawn from books written by linguists, most readers would accept them at face value. However, upon close examination we can see that the quoted sentences are very misleading. To illustrate this point, I need you to perform a brief experiment. Please read the following sentence aloud: "He sick." It's important to say the sentence aloud. Now, please read "He's sick" aloud, taking care to say it as you normally would in conversation. If you repeat this process a few times, again making sure to say both sentences at your normal rate of speech, you will notice that they sound identical. Thus, from the standpoint of conversation, this is an example of phonological neutralization which is not immediately apparent from the written comparison of "He sick" versus "He's sick." I should be quick to point out that a sentence where the verb did not begin with /s/ would serve to illustrate Dillard's point better (for example, "He coming" or "She pretty").

If linguists can, albeit unintentionally, mislead their readers in this way, imagine the difficulty for those who rely on the linguists' judgment for educational or other social purposes. The preceding example stands out here because it focuses on *is*, but it is by no means special when compared to the vast oversimplification of black speech in most of the historical literature. Returning, then, to the significance of *is* within a historical survey, I have suggested that we

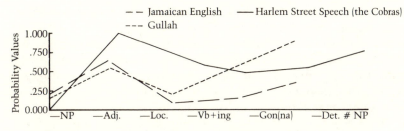

2. Variation for *is* absence in Jamaican English, Gullah, and Harlem street speech

are looking at complementary hypotheses. The reader might properly wonder how this could be; after all, how could *is* and the lack of *is* exist as historical renditions without direct opposition? The answer lies in the gradual historical changes that have occurred.[2] Elsewhere (Baugh 1980), I demonstrate that *is* usage in street speech has ancestral ties both to the Gullah dialect of the Sea Islands and to Jamaican English. Recalling my observation that many of the early creolist scholars searched for monographs from the slave trade in their efforts to reconstruct the protolanguage of slaves, it occurred to me that a new procedure might benefit from a direct comparison of contemporary oral linguistic behavior in disparate black English communities. This is exactly what I did; by comparing the speech of Harlem teens, the Gullah dialect, and Jamaican English, a parallel pattern for the deletion of *is* was revealed. This is illustrated in figure 2.

The categories at the bottom of each graph identify specific linguistic environments that were measured for *is* usage in these three communities—and the similarities are much too great to reflect only historical coincidence. This is especially true when white American dialects are compared to this pattern. The best evidence that is now available subsequently suggests that a complex pattern of historical, social, and linguistic forces has influenced ongoing changes in black street speech. My own research suggests historical linguistic roots that link black street speech with Jamaican creole and Scots-Irish dialects.

For years educators hoped that linguists could solve the historical riddle of black street speech, but, considering the diversity of opinion that exists, practitioners were torn between two highly plausible extremes. I tend to agree with Wolfram's observation

2. I would especially like to thank William Labov and Ralph Fasold for pointing me in the right direction with their pioneering studies.

(1974) that an accurate historical picture is not necessary to formulate a clear analysis of street speech today. While it made good sense twenty years ago to consider this historical debate as part of the educational picture, the final analysis shows that contemporary speech patterns are only part of an intricate pedagogical picture. I would argue that, in spite of the benefits that historical reflection can give us, the evidence is still quite scant. In addition, we have ready access to the street speech that thrives in our own inner cities, and it is from these cities that my study draws its life.

3
Street Speech and Formal Speech: Linguistic Survival in Black and White Societies

The previous historical backdrop provides the necessary depth to allow us to understand the unique social and linguistic problems that face modern black street speakers. As indicated at the outset, black America is not a monoculture. Different interactional strategies are employed by blacks with highly diversified backgrounds. A common denominator nevertheless remains: most blacks are required to function in two societies—one black, the other white. Black street speech is therefore highly functional in the black community, and, from a linguistic point of view, it is equal to any other living language. However, because of the stigma that is still borne by black English—in so many places—black children are taught, if not at home then in school, that the larger mainstream society demands a more "educated" manner of speaking. It is mainly this combination of an oral history with the negative attitudes toward vernacular black dialects that makes this topic so interesting, especially from a linguistic perspective.

When a language has a long-standing written tradition, as in the case of standard English, contemporary generations of speakers come to view the prescriptive grammar as correct, and mere speech is seen as being less than correct. This perception is dominant in societies where the official standard is swaddled with strong emotional and nationalistic overtones. The social or geographical isolation that gave rise to dialect separation tends to be reinforced when speakers interact across dialect lines. Even in situations where generations of nonstandard speakers have gravitated toward the standard, this process is seldom completed to the point where all traces of the native dialect are erased.

Several linguistic strategies have been developed to cope with the pressure of having to survive in two cultures. The behavior that is rewarded in white society is often alien to vernacular black contexts—the opposite of course holds true. Because my study took me to the people, in all types of social contexts, several consultants commented specifically on the nature of black-white relations; their comments are far more vivid than my own:

> J.: Do you feel the situation has improved, y' know, between blacks and whites?
>
> R.: Naw . . . it's like, well, I think the majority of black people are just not comfortable around a majority of whites. Like, dig, you can't just be yourself—y' understand? See, like if a brother gets on my case I can tell blood, "Hey motherfucker you can kiss my ass," and the brother can deal with that—y' know, take it in stride—cause he know where I'm comin from. But you can't be tellin no white dude that. If a white dude does somethin you gotta play it real cool, cause otherwise it's just gon explode. So, I would say no; cause the majority of black people just can't be themselves.

The linguistic consequences of this are fairly obvious but might be a little misleading from the preceding quote. For example, many whites assume that cursing is essential to black street speech, but, while there is typically greater usage of curse words, members of the vernacular culture filter this information through a slightly different process:

> J.: So what happened when you talked to him [a young white coworker who was taking classes to become a welder]?
>
> J.T.: Well, it pissed me off that the dude was steady cursin; I mean, whenever the dude be talkin to the brothers it was "motherfucker this" and "motherfucker that." They say we be doin all the cursin, but this white boy cursed hisself up a storm. See, like a brother know how to use the same words *and not curse you at all*, but this white boy ain't learned that.

Abrahams, among others, has observed that the amount of cursing and slang fluctuates depending on the social context. Young black men in the presence of women display respect by toning down their talk. And, within the vernacular culture, this contextual display of dialect styles conforms to systematic patterns of linguistic behavior. Highly ritualized speech acts, like the well-known dozens or shuckin' and jivin' (discussed below), are similarly reserved for special circumstances. These subjects have been discussed elsewhere at length, and I have little to add to the good work that is available. However, there is a neglected perspective, one that looks in detail at the actual linguistic behavior as it adjusts to various contexts in day-to-day life. From an analytic point of view this is tedious work and is therefore performed by relatively few linguists; but, in my case, I feel that it is the responsibility of black scholars to establish the standards for this kind of research. My study is thus cast in the conservative tradition of classical linguistic descriptions.

In much the same manner that Boas and Sapir recorded native American languages firsthand, I went to the streets of Los Angeles, Philadelphia, Chicago, and Texas to document the black American dialects there. In chapters 4 and 5 I will outline my procedures in greater detail; at this stage let it suffice to say that street speech fluctuates depending on the social situation.

In order to subdivide the data into different categories, it was necessary to develop a grid for comparative purposes. Recalling my desire to utilize the precision that is offered by linguistic description, I was careful to choose social criteria that could be specified for all the evidence. The initial categories are illustrated in figure 3.

Familiar (Frequent Contact)	Unfamiliar (Occasional Contact)	
TYPE 1 Familiar Exchange	TYPE 2 Intracommunity Contact	Members of Black Street Culture
TYPE 3 Intercommunity Exchange	TYPE 4 Outsider Contact	Outsiders to Black Street Culture

3. Speech event subdivisions

The horizontal division corresponds to whether speakers are—or are not—members of the vernacular black culture, where familiarity among power equals prevails. In familiar speech events, the participants must be so well acquainted that the interaction or the mere presence of others does not constitute a formal gathering. It is important to recall that formality depends on your point of view: what is formal for workers may be very informal from the perspective of their bosses; the same holds true in student-teacher relationships and in almost any other situation where power is displayed. With this flexibility in mind, then, I have concentrated on the impact of the social context as it affects black speech styles. The vertical division represents the boundary between familiars and non-familiars. For the most part interaction among intimates involved familiar conversations, where the participants were well acquainted as power equals. However, in type 3 speech events, for example, between an employer and an employee, familiarity was not automatically associated with intimacy.

Of course, the degree of familiarity lies within the perception of each participant. Since I recognized the difficulty of trying to determine how each speaker viewed every conversation, the preceding speech event subdivisions were provided to test prevailing trends and should not be seen as rigid categories for (in)formality. There is a great degree of reliability in this procedure, however, because—with the advantage of long-term study—the development of personal relationships can be taken into account. Speech event types, then, are identified as follows:

Type 1   depicts speech events that have familiar participants, all of whom are natives of the black vernacular culture. They also share long-term relationships, which tend to be close-knit and self-supporting.

Type 2   represents speech events where participants are not well acquainted but are members of the black vernacular culture.

Type 3   indicates speech events where participants are well acquainted but black street speech is not shared; solidarity may or may not exist between any two or more individuals.

Type 4   corresponds to speech events where participants are not familiar nor is black street speech common to all.

The precedent for divisions of this kind, in spite of their admitted limitations, is well known in classical linguistic studies (compare Brown and Gilman 1960). When I first developed these four speech event types, I thought the racial boundary (that is, vernacular membership) would be the strongest force between formal and informal speech—the final results proved to be a bit more complicated. First, to illustrate the utility of these divisions, especially when collecting evidence from various consultants, let us review some of the well-known oral rituals and the circumstances where they are most likely to appear.

The case of the dozens is well attested. Males, and occasionally females, hurl ritual insults at one another, involving their mothers as the target of the verbal assault. These insults are most likely to occur in type 1 speech events, where insiders are well acquainted. It could be very dangerous to engage in this in type 2 speech events, because there is no reliable way to determine the reaction of unfamiliars. The dozens are therefore reserved for situations that are almost always exclusive to black males who are intimates. Another oral ritual, one that is far more complicated, would be the situation where shuckin' and jivin' prevail.

Shuckin' and jivin' can occur in all four speech event types. Some additional background may be useful. The economic and social oppression of slavery, where blacks were severely punished for slight or major conflicts with whites, created a climate where it was necessary to devise communication strategies that allowed blacks to preserve their self-respect while not offending the whites interacting with them. The social situation has of course changed a great deal through the years, but shuckin' and jivin' are still common practices in contemporary black vernacular speech events.

In chapter 5, other linguistic processes will be outlined in greater detail. The oral rituals, however, like the dozens, shuckin' and jivin', rappin', and so on, are illustrative of speech acts with specific functions. The newer long-term data now show that social contexts play a direct role in the frequency with which vernacular street speech or more formal black English is used. The social pressures and history that we have already considered cast a hazy light on the full style-shifting process, because many of the changes take place beneath thresholds of conscious awareness. Nevertheless, although my consultants were not always able to pinpoint the exact nature of their linguistic adjustments, they were well aware of the process. Their views, once again, state the case with vivid clarity:

> J.: Have you come in contact with any other situations where you could see the difference [in dialect]?
>
> R.: O.K. . . . yesterday . . . O.K. . . . in my apartment building there are some New York poor white people . . . O.K. . . . now, I know they didn't live the best of their lives . . . like most whites . . . O.K. They can relate more than the California white person . . . let's say like that . . . O.K.?
>
> So, I'm sitting over there talking to them . . . right? Two of my girlfriends come in, right? . . . they come in, they come to their house [the whites' house] . . . right? O.K. . . . we introduce everybody . . . I would sit there and see them trying to make the black girls comfortable when it wasn't really necessary. Y' know . . . they want . . . they try to make lots of conversation, lots of laughter . . . and that's not necessary.
>
> J.: So what did the sisters do? How did they handle it?
>
> R.: The sisters . . . they felt . . . I could sit there, I saw them . . . the way they felt, like, they was saying to theyself, like . . . yeah, here some more white people trying to make us feel comfortable when it's not really necessary.
>
> J.: No . . . but how was their reaction?
>
> R.: O.K. . . . their reaction was kinda like . . . sit back . . . and watch the show . . . cause if you get up and try to dance

with them [the whites], then they gonna step out and watch
you act a fool . . . and so, when you go around white people,
you either gon be on stage, or you gon be in the audience . . . y'
know? . . . 'n you got to sit back . . . *say little to nothing,* or
you gotta be up there, which I call making a fool out of yourself; yackity yackity yack . . . they already think they know
too much about you anyway . . . y' know . . . and if they see
you up there . . . you just a mouthpiece . . . most whites don't
figure blacks think too well.

 J.: What kind of change did you go through?

 R.: Well . . . for me . . . it was even hard for me *because the
conversations were different.*

 J.: What do you mean?

 R.: O.K. . . . I have to sit . . . right? I'm in the middle cause I
know them both. They are both my friends . . . like . . . this.
O.K., on this hand, *I have to talk to them* [the whites] *one way
and then I have to turn right back around and talk to them*
[the black girls] *another way . . . and try to keep him* [the
white man] *from feeling left out of this conversation, and the
girls from feeling left out in the other conversation* . . . so . . .
it's kind of hard to sit in the middle of a situation like that.

 This appraisal is remarkably accurate when compared with the
data: significant adjustments are made as blacks try to modify their
behavior to suit various situations. It would be wrong to suggest that
all adjustments across racial lines are deferential. We must keep in
mind that an individual's self-image and world view can—and often
do—result in different reactions to the same stimuli, even for empa-
thetic members of black street culture. Some will adopt a hostile
stance, while others will simply ignore whites or choose to take
these rare contacts as an opportunity for philosophical debate. Assuming, then, that social circumstances play a role in the type of
speech blacks use—which, again, may seem obvious at first blush—
the purely linguistic question boils down to the specific changes
that take place.

 Two major issues should therefore be taken into account: the
history of slavery and oppression prevented the normal transition to
standard English, and the modern descendants of slaves still find
that they need to exist in two societies. I am, of course, excluding
blacks who have little or no contact with street culture; their situation is better suited to another book. Black readers will nevertheless
need to be aware of how some typical standard English speakers
view this situation.

Access to standard English for blacks has been an uphill climb since the birth of the nation. Many white Americans, especially those whose ancestors came from non-English-speaking countries, arriving in New York or Chicago as poor immigrants, often tend to feel that most blacks are not really trying to make it on their own. It is all too common to hear whites say, "I'm tired of working and paying my taxes to support these people who are taking a free ride on the welfare system." This perception, whether distorted or accurate, spills over into other stereotypical attitudes as well, many of which are reinforced when street speech is interpreted as proof that blacks don't want to change themselves "for the better." Fortunately, because I conducted interviews with white college-educated consultants, I have anecdotal evidence which illustrates this perceptual paradox.

The following, stated to me during one of my lectures on the general tpoic of black speech, is indicative of how many nonblacks view the problem. The speaker is a fifty-four-year-old professor of economics at a prestigious university:

> My grandparents came here from Poland, and when my grandfather arrived in Chicago he only had three dollars in his pocket. He went out and bought some fruit; he sold that fruit for a profit and bought more fruit. My people lived through the roughest part of the depression and we had to pick ourselves up by our bootstraps again. Now, considering that we [his relatives from Poland] came here with nothing and worked ourselves into a good life after only three generations, how is it that blacks—who have been here for over four hundred years—can't do the same thing?

While this line of reasoning sounds plausible to so many people, especially to the descendants of immigrants who suffered (brief) discrimination and economic deprivation, white immigrants have always been allowed to melt into the pot relatively quickly, while nonwhite populations in the United States have always had to melt at a slower rate.

Keeping our focus on the related impact on language, one of the attributes that made blacks attractive as slaves was our overt visible contrast to white indentured servants, which throughout our history has been an additional blockade to entering mainstream society. Also, while many nonblacks consider poverty to be a common point of social entry, poverty alone does not reflect the special barriers that blacks have faced considering their unique linguistic history. As indicated in chapter 2, most white immigrants came to

America from societies with a long-standing written tradition, and they were able to maintain the language of their homeland until future generations—learning local standard English and acquiring their education in white schools—were able to enter society on a competitive footing. Descendants of slaves, on the other hand, by virtue of being denied the use of their African tongue, were forced to use a pidginized English. Add, once more, the historical fact that it was illegal to teach slaves to read and write, and the likelihood of access to the linguistic mainstream diminishes rapidly.

As has always been the case in the United States, and in most other nations, those who are in positions of political power and social control dictate the standards of linguistic acceptability. This has forced unilateral accommodation on the part of blacks and other minorities, as far as the direction of linguistic change is concerned. This is not a value judgment; rather, it is a statement of historical fact. By contrast, if the linguistic demands were truly equal throughout the society, many standard speakers would likewise be faced with the considerable task of learning a second dialect or language. Under the present social circumstances such a consideration seems absurd, although egalitarian. Many standard English speakers state the case as follows: "If people want to live in the United States, then they had better learn good English—if they ever hope to succeed." The implications of this opinion, while true in our contemporary context, take on a hypocritical tone in the historical context of the birth of the nation. Few people adopted the philosophy of learning native American languages, to say nothing of the massive crimes against native people.

To return to the situation at hand, the nature of black street speech can be clarified with help from sociologists. Goffman, in two works that touch on the topic at hand, defines social situations and performance teams:

> I would define a social situation as an environment of mutual monitoring possibilities, anywhere within which an individual will find himself accessible to the naked senses of all others who are "present," and similarly find them accessible to him. (1972:63)

> I will use the terms "performance team" or, in short, "team" to refer to any set of individuals who co-operate in staging a single routine. (1959:79)

Taken together, these definitions illustrate the special problems that affect most blacks in their interaction within and across racial lines.

For the sake of illustration let us assume, albeit falsely, that blacks and whites comprise two performance teams. It would then be a fairly simple matter for interactants to determine if their immediate circumstances included their team or if nonteam members were present.

The concepts of teams and situations therefore tend to complement each other when speech events are under consideration. When I first began this project, I thought that the division between black vernacular community members and nonmembers (illustrated by the horizontal division in figure 3) would correlate with the dominant changes in linguistic behavior, but the final results suggest that familiarity plays a more strategic role.

Since I was well acquainted with all the black consultants, it was a fairly simple matter for me to determine the relationships between speakers in any of the interviews. Our linguistic objective, however, being derived from these social divisions, has been to determine the extent to which immediate interlocutors affect each other's linguistic behavior. Goffman's sense of performance teams is very appropriate when we analyze the actual behavior of people in several social settings.

The importance of my concentration on adults, as well as the benefits of long-term research, is amplified when compared to previous assessments of adult black speech. A related issue focuses on how street speech is transmitted from one generation to the next:

> This comparatively archaic character of the speech of the younger children—always those who are beyond the stage of language acquisition, of "learning to talk"—is sociolinguistically perhaps the most exciting factor in Black English. It is no mystic process, at any rate; the older the child grows, the more he has to adjust his language to something like mainstream culture. Linguists have long known that the popular metaphor about "mother tongue" is almost meaningless; beyond the earliest beginnings, the child learns most from his peer group. As a matter of fact, current studies of language acquisition minimize the factor of imitating the parents in the case of any young language learner. Parents may not like it, but they really have little influence on the behavior of their children. (Dillard 1972:236)

Dillard is not alone in his assumption. Most researchers on this topic, including those studying children, adolescents, and adults, primarily recorded or observed type 4 speech events. This should not be viewed as a criticism, due to the pioneering nature of their work, but such limited exposure gives the impression that youths are somehow most responsible for the preservation and use of black street speech. I would like to suggest a different scenario. For example, children do not migrate—thereby preserving the vernacular dialect—unless at the behest of adults, nor do children have the linguistic dexterity to shift from one dialect to another with the ease, experience, or proficiency of adults in the same community. This would help explain why adults are seen as being more standard, while children who are interviewed under similar conditions are considered to be the most authentic speakers of the vernacular dialect.[1]

In the next chapter, I will outline the procedures that I developed to approach my consultants. The data took years to collect, and the time spent in parks, homes, and local bars eroded the initial barriers between me and the residents. As far as style shifting is concerned, Goffman's concepts of teams and situations are essential to a full appreciation of why blacks modify their speech. A complementary tool, developed by Hymes, looks at the ethnography of speaking for any speech community. Hymes (1974) has demonstrated that every speaker, regardless of language or social circumstance, will share universal properties with every other speaker. Every typical conversation consists of a sender, a receiver, a topic of discussion, a code (that is, language and dialect), a channel of communication (for example, mouth to ear or telegraph lines), and a setting for the speech event.

When street speech is viewed from an ethnographic perspective, we find that the dialect is modified depending on the immediate evaluations of the participants. In other words, every face-to-face conversation takes place under circumstances that can be defined as a social situation, using Goffman's definition. Depending upon the social relationships of the participants, as well as such other factors as the topic of discussion, everyone will monitor their register of speaking along an (in)formal continuum. As suggested previously, all speakers have a range of formal to informal speech, but adult street speech is characterized by a greater degree of linguistic adjustment. This should not suggest that the most formal varieties of black speech are identical to white standard dialects. Often black

1. Another reason why the creolists focused on the speech of black youths was motivated by the desire to compare parallels between child language development and the development of new (that is, pidgin and creole) languages. The end result has nevertheless diminished concern for the role of black adults in the life and utility of street speech.

vernacular speakers overshoot the mark when they produce their standard rendition, thereby making hypercorrections—that is, the utterance reflects an overgeneralization of the standard English equivalent (for example, *pickted* versus *picked*). Hypercorrection, an important dimension of style shifting in street speech, has been discussed at some length by Labov and his colleagues (1968), Wolfram (1969), and others. The significant difference between hypercorrect forms, as opposed to other features of nonstandard street speech, is that they regularize the *standard* grammatical and/or phonological paradigms.

From the standpoint of the standard speaker, however, hypercorrect forms will still constitute a "mistake." The nature of this linguistic difference is nevertheless important when we also consider forms like distributive *be* and stressed *been* (see chapter 6), as opposed to hypercorrect uses like *lookted* and *teses*. Educators will be especially interested in this process, because not all differences between street speech and standard English are derived from the same source.

By looking closely at the type of speech that is produced under different circumstances, we can get a better image of black street speech, as well as the social forces that affect everyday usage. Readers who are not familiar with black speech may have experienced a similar phenomenon through a process known as dialect leveling. When two individuals who speak different dialects come together, there may be a tendency to adjust speech in the direction of other interlocutors. I should point out that attitudinal preferences can play a major role in the extent—and direction—of dialect leveling. Many of my colleagues in Texas have observed that they will use one (formal) register when working at the university; but, when they return home to rural areas, they tend to adopt their home dialect after a short period of time. In fact, the process can even be observed during long-distance telephone conversations.

I would like to suggest that style shifting and dialect leveling are quite natural. Giles and Powesland's work (1975) on accommodation theory outlines this very process in far more thorough detail. All people are more comfortable when they are interacting with others who share common norms, and linguistic performance is one of the most important criteria for establishing rapport. When dialect differences arise, people typically make adjustments—whether slight or severe—to accommodate their interlocutors. Among power equals, where no strong attitudes prevail, there is a tendency for mutual adjustment. When power is imbalanced, however, as has so often been the case for whites and blacks in America, the onus of adjustment lies with the person who does not hold power. In fact, when blacks do not attempt to adjust to more formal white speech, especially in school or in court appearances, their maintenance of the vernacular is often perceived as hostile behavior or insubordination. Logic should tell us that these same perceptions are based on social expectations, not on a full appreciation of the linguistic facts that confront street speakers in a standard English world.

Whites would be hard-pressed to achieve their same levels of success if they were first required to learn another English dialect, say, impeccable British English. There is regional tolerance for variation in white speech; and, as long as there are no economic consequences for speaking with an accent, that accent can prevail, albeit regionally. But black street speech has been stained with the folk mythology that equates it with illiteracy, poverty, and other trappings of prejudicial isolation. Most white Americans therefore assume that those who speak standardized English are trying to improve themselves. This may be true; it will nevertheless be a unilateral enterprise for black street speakers as long as the standards are dictated by and for people who acquire standard English as their native dialect.

Because black English style shifts are shrouded with this complex fabric of social, political, and linguistic facts, it has not been easy to examine them. I have chosen to collect evidence from black street speakers themselves. As mentioned, this is a time-consuming process, and some black scholars have chosen to use their own intuitions to illustrate the structure of vernacular black English. In many cases these "vernacular" renditions are produced by highly educated individuals who, like myself, have been extensively exposed to standard English as part of their education and training. If there is an ironic aspect to my research, it lies in the fact that the skills required of all scholars demand fluency with the relevant standard language. This same process has, in turn, at least in my case, clouded my intuitions with respect to dialect boundaries. Thus, while there are increasing numbers of black scholars working on several minority-related issues, this population is still quite sparse when compared to the majority of blacks who are outside the academic arena—by choice, chance, or design. Moreover, because black street speech is known to be stigmatized outside of the home community, the examination of style shifts can be a very ticklish problem if data collection is not handled with care. In spite of these problems, I would argue strongly that the most reliable evidence on street speech cannot be found by listening to the linguistic experts—regardless of race—and I include myself in this group. Rather, we must learn about the language from the isolated population which has little or no access to the academic community. The dynamics of street speech can be derived only from life in the home community, and ultimately this requires the cooperation of black people themselves.

It is one thing to recognize the need to gather data from representative consultants, but it is another matter altogether to get the job done. Gaining the cooperation of street speakers can be complicated. The upper and lower classes in western societies tend to be the most difficult groups to approach in urban fieldwork, because both groups are closed, although for different reasons. Since street speakers have typically encountered negative reactions to their behavior when they venture into mainstream domains, it is quite understandable that their suspicions are aroused by outsiders who suddenly appear, not to mention outsiders who also desire to record their conversations. As a black American I understood this problem and tried to account for it in this study. In a broader context, Labov (1972a) has defined this problem as the observer's paradox; we hope to record data that are authentic, that is, the colloquial speech, but the recording process itself can formalize—and consequently distort—the data. We see some artifacts of this problem in Dillard's observation that black adults tend toward standard English. My experience has been that the majority of adults have simply attained a level of style shifting that is not fully developed during childhood and adolescence; again, there are exceptions.

Before we look directly at the procedures that I have developed, we should first consider another paradox—that between deductive and inductive studies in linguistics. When linguistic science first emerged as an autonomous discipline, early in the century, most work was inductive in its orientation. Scholars derived their analyses, in the American structuralist tradition, based on in-depth examinations of actual conversations. As Chomsky has remarked on several occasions, the practice of relying exclusively on inductive data places severe restrictions on linguists, implying that one cannot complete an analysis unless conversations are first collected as utterances. What if the linguist was interested in studying a form that rarely appeared in speech? Would the science be shackled until specific sentences were produced? The source of linguistic data is the main concern here.

Thus, in much the same manner that Einstein performed thought experiments to develop his theory of relativity, Chomsky conducted thought experiments in linguistics to devise his models for generative grammar. There can be no question regarding his contribution to linguistic science; however, in the wake of his efforts many linguists have simply neglected the theoretical value of inductive studies. Chomsky discussed the implications for black English research directly in *Language and Responsibility*:

> The study of various dialects certainly falls squarely within linguistics. But I do not see in what way the study of ghetto dialects differs from the study of dialects of university trained speakers, from a purely linguistic point of view. . . . The study of Black English, from a linguistic point of view, is on a par with the study of Korean or of American Indian languages, or of the difference between the English of Cambridge, England and Cambridge, Massachusetts. (1977:54, 55)

With all due respect to Chomsky and his tremendous contribution to the entire discipline, certain underlying assumptions in his remarks are very misleading. In order to conduct the kind of thought experiments for language that he advocates, linguists must have access to well-formed sentences—regardless of their inductive or deductive source—to develop an adequate theory of language. When this enterprise is restricted to the standard dialects of intellectuals or to isolated examples from single informants of more "exotic" languages, one might easily assume—as Chomsky has—that the study of ghetto dialects is on a par with the study of university-trained speakers. This opinion does not take sociolinguistic realities into account. Linguistic intuitions can easily become clouded when social pressures, like being told that one speaks "bad" English, influence grammatical judgments.

University-trained scholars typically speak standard languages, for the most part those with long-standing prescriptive traditions. Thus, their idealization of linguistic facts through thought experiments tends to be constrained by notions of correctness which, for educated speakers, are closely associated with what street speakers consider to be bookish English. The genuine problem that we encounter, which I would characterize as a theoretical paradox, is the fact that the idealization of linguistic intuitions must be based on a keen sense of what is grammatical and what is not. And, in pursuit of an adequate linguistic theory, scholars have tested the parameters of grammaticality and semantic change by closely examining idealized and highly complex linguistic structures. This practice is useful, nevertheless, and will of course continue in spite of the limitations that are inherent with deductive methods.

However, studying black street speech is not the same as studying university-trained speakers because the history of the dialects differs, and this has distorted the intuitions of the most reliable consultants, that is, with respect to where the true grammatical boundaries lie. For years well-intended public school teachers, knowing that street speech is stigmatized within the mainstream culture, have "corrected" the speech of black children, thereby giving them the impression that nonstandard speech is wrong when compared to standardized dialects. So, while linguists might have the sophistication to appreciate that nonstandard utterances are grammatical (for example, "It ain't no way all y'all gon go"), most American English speakers claim that such sentences are ungrammatical (that is, ill formed in Chomsky's sense). The student of ghetto dialects is therefore faced with the burden of reeducating a large segment of the population—both black and white—before arriving at the stage where nonstandard sentences would be considered to be just as grammatical as their bookish counterparts. Most readers will recognize that we are far from this point.

This background serves to amplify the theoretical paradox, because we need to determine who is in an adequate position to state what is and what is not grammatical for black street speech. Considering Chomsky's position on the subject, we would first look for individuals who could reliably construct idealized nonstandard utterances and then examine these intuitions in connection with prevailing linguistic theories. In my case, as a black man who encountered strong negative reactions to street speech at every stage of my educational training, I recognize that it is nearly impossible to find an individual who has both an adequate appreciation of linguistic theory and unbiased intuitions regarding the grammaticality of street speech. Educators do not, and in my opinion should not, let their students go through school without trying to expose them to the standard language that is required in professional fields, but this very process can easily cloud intuitions regarding dialect boundaries.

Moreover, the first detailed studies of black dialects were conducted by white scholars, who could not claim access to native intuitions about vernacular black speech; they had to maintain an inductive orientation. White scholars collected large corpora in order to determine the linguistic nature of black dialects. If we take Chomsky's observations at face value, then we readily see that a new double standard emerges with respect to access to the linguistic facts—and this problem is in turn amplified by the relative paucity of black scholars working on this topic.

For example, let us assume for the moment that—rather than spending several years collecting data—I used my linguistic training to develop an intuitive (that is, deductive) account of black street speech; I would be assuming the license to describe a dialect that few other linguists would know anything about. White scholars interested in this subject are obligated to carefully collect evidence and conduct their studies in an inductive manner. Black scholars, on the other hand, once equipped with an adequate linguistic theory, might be given the opportunity to conduct deductive studies, based on their presumed familiarity with their native dialect. I would therefore argue, as strongly as I possibly can, that Chomsky has—in this instance—oversimplified and overstated the case. Historical realities and educational Darwinism have affected our ability to gain ready access to reliable evidence on black street speech. The kind of idealization to which Chomsky refers is reserved for the elite dialects of scholars or for limited evidence from isolated speakers of lesser-known languages.[1]

In my case, I chose not to claim unbiased intuitions about street speech because of several personal factors, the most important of which has been my education and the subsequent standardization of my speech. I have therefore chosen to conduct my studies in the black community, and this process simply takes time. Its procedures draw on several disciplines, including linguistics, ethnography, and sociology. I conducted the fieldwork as a participant observer through a civil service job; I worked as a lifeguard in black neighborhoods in Los Angeles and Philadelphia. Although black lifeguards are a rarity, largely for socioeconomic reasons, I was fortunate enough to swim on my high school team. I had therefore been a lifeguard before developing a professional interest in linguistics.

My first objective, once I became interested in pursuing this topic, was to gradually introduce my research in the hope of meeting prospective consultants. As a graduate student, I felt the available work on black English was derived from two major sources: firsthand studies of black speech acts (see Abrahams 1976; Kochman 1972, 1981; Mitchell-Kernan 1969; Labov 1972b; Folb 1980) and

---

1. For the sake of clarity and contrast I have stated the extreme positions here; however, as most linguists know, the actual situation is not so cut-and-dried. There are several indirect methods of studying linguistic intuitions, and they are well established in various branches of the field.

studies based on children or adolescents (see Dillard 1972; Labov et al. 1968; Baratz and Shuy 1969). My objective was initially to continue the practice of recording adolescents, and the public pool proved to be an excellent location to meet teens during their summer vacation. But my interest turned to adults because several situations arose where conversations among them were interrupted by outsiders to the area, primarily the white supervisors who were assigned to visit each pool periodically. Just as children sit rigidly in their seats when the school principal walks into the classroom, street speakers shift styles when they perceive a formal situation. In this case I was observing sophisticated linguistic maneuvers in action. The problem was getting the adaptations on tape. In other words, it was necessary to find some way to overcome the observer's paradox.

A momentary regression will clarify my situation. Two previous studies on black speech have exhibited what I refer to as ethnosensitive fieldwork. Ethnosensitivity requires the fieldworker to collect the data, in this instance linguistic interviews, in such a manner that the values and cultural orientation of the native consultants are taken into account. When I first used this term (Baugh 1979), I was concentrating on the special problems facing black English research, but since that time others have applied the principle to all types of firsthand fieldwork with human subjects. In the case of street speech, however, fieldworkers must proceed with judicious caution, because suspicions can easily be aroused and social violations— once committed—are often hard to overcome.

Since I had a full-time seasonal job and had worked at both the Philadelphia and the Los Angeles sites two years prior to the fieldwork, I became known to a lot of local residents. Being black proved to be important to my fieldwork, because I was already aware of the double standards that blacks must live by. No one wants to be made to look like a fool, yet in racial confrontation after racial confrontation the linguistic hurdles are typically the most frustrating. In the home setting, on the other hand, where people feel they can relax without being judged, the vernacular is the norm and meets every expressive need.

Some linguists actually advocate the use of surreptitious recordings for such ticklish situations, but I am not among them. With the proper ethnosensitive procedures, it is possible to explain your objectives in ways that demonstrate the utility of the work for the consultants themselves. John Lewis was largely responsible for collecting much of Labov's black English data in Harlem. Having analyzed most of Lewis' data (see Baugh 1980), I was struck by the fact that he was aware of the boundaries of acceptable verbal challenges, while taking care to minimize confrontations. In the black community it would be difficult to pretend not to hold opinions on various topics of local and national importance. Hymes (1974) has observed this fact; he notes that informants want to share in a quid pro quo exchange. Unilateral discussions are often perceived as unfair—the consultants do a lot of talking, but the conversation is shallow unless there is give-and-take. It has been my experience that genuine interaction is based upon an appreciation of the topics of local and personal interest. Wolfram, a white scholar, used another technique: playing pickup basketball in black neighborhoods. Having grown up in Philadelphia, he had developed a sense of street wiseness, knowing that he would have to earn respect athletically before he could be trusted on a personal level. Ethnosensitivity therefore requires acute self-awareness in addition to an in-depth knowledge of the community under investigation.

In my first year of fieldwork I always carried a tape recorder, which is common for black men in the city. However, upon close observation, some people noticed that I never listened to music. This would come up on occasions when men gathered and compared their "boxes" (that is, their tape recorders). Since most were interested in their music, their boxes were equipped with radios and large speakers. My machine appeared to be quite small by comparison. The observation that I never listened to my tape recorder became an important aspect of the study, because it set the stage for my being able to introduce the research. It is critical to appreciate that prospective consultants made the observation that I did not play music, and, upon their inquiry—which was not solicited by me—I was able to mention my goal of recording oral histories about life in black America. Most other fieldworkers initiate conversations by requesting permission to record. Some of my best street consultants would have resisted or rejected such an approach. However, because I waited until they had questioned me first, I was able to introduce my objectives without seeming pushy. This is an important component to the research, because privacy is highly prized in the vernacular black culture, and I knew that any violation of this unwritten law would diminish my credibility and possibly ruin my chances of getting any recordings at all.

Ultimately the question of sampling comes down to a personal level: the fieldworker and each consultant establish mutually convenient times to meet; handshakes, greetings, and other salutations are exchanged; and careful steps are taken to overcome the inevitable preliminary nervousness that consultants experience upon seeing microphones and tape recorders. The value of the present corpus derives from my dual role in the community, with primary emphasis on my status as a lifeguard, which led to extensive contacts and personal interactions that provided natural settings for conducting the desired linguistic interviews. Because of my extensive contacts in the community, I had the uncommon advantage of discussing my linguistic interests in broad terms whenever the topic fit into the natural flow of conversation. I say "uncommon advantage" here because most other analyses, even those based in black English communities, were gathered under severe time constraints, which would make it even more difficult to establish anything resembling a stable rapport. There are, of course, some noteworthy exceptions, as illustrated in Folb's long-term study (1980) of black teen speech and Stack's study (1974) of black kinship networks.

Imagine a situation where new coworkers come to know one another better, establishing friendships and/or hostilities along capricious social and personal lines. It is very natural for discussions of a highly personal nature to increase as familiarity grows. This brings us back to the point about ethnosensitivity discussed earlier. The student of black English will probably have little success collecting colloquial speech through direct inquiries that are not framed in terms of the consultants' cultural perspectives. This general principle may hold true for many other speech communities as well, especially those with oral traditions that are highly stigmatized. We subsequently find that many of the best sociolinguistic interviews come from fieldworkers who are aware of their consultants' local interests, values, and general social norms.

Turning, then, to my specific situation, it was—and still is—my belief that most adult black street speakers will initially resist the idea of being interviewed in a variety of situations by anyone, black or white, whom they do not know well. This point is easily understood if we think in terms of a simple formula which assumes, for the majority, that people are more likely to be trusting of others whom they know well and that trust can be established only over a period of time.

My general approach was therefore very flexible, because I would simply wait for prospective consultants to inquire about my "off-the-job" interests. The details of this method will be discussed in greater depth momentarily, but, at this stage, it is essential to appreciate the significance of the waiting strategy. The natural inquisition that accompanies new social contacts as well as the exchange of past experiences are authentic in the real world. I simply extended this same procedure to any prospective consultant whom I met. The authenticity of the vernacular data has been greatly enhanced as a result of this initiation by consultants. During the final two years of the Los Angeles study, I lived in the local community, thereby becoming known to many area residents.

Most of the consultants in the sample are literate, although it would be wrong to suggest that they all have a strong command of reading and writing skills. Nevertheless, because I did not want to jeopardize the informal atmosphere that had been growing, consultants were not requested to perform any reading or writing tasks. Since some of the best street speakers have had minimal contact with standard English, any request for reading and writing could have been embarrassing. Most Americans, regardless of background, are generally presumed to know how to read and write once they reach adulthood.

As stated, during the first year of the fieldwork a waiting strategy was necessary because I had no preestablished entrée in the area. In subsequent years, however, some consultants helped locate new consultants and in two cases even conducted interviews in my absence. In every instance consultants were aware of being recorded and knew that this research was being used for multiple purposes. When prospective consultants asked me what I did when I was not a lifeguard, the conversation would focus on my college career in California and Pennsylvania, and we would discuss my interests in studying black American culture through oral histories.

Most blacks in the United States know quite a lot about black history from a variety of sources. When the general topic was mentioned, most people were interested in knowing more. On those occasions when more detailed discussion followed, I generally indicated that blacks were in a difficult social position, compared to most other immigrants from countries with long-standing written traditions. I then indicated that this special dilemma for blacks accentuated the value of our oral history and that, unless serious efforts were made to record individual histories, the true values of black American culture could not be fully recognized; all these statements are, of course, true.

When I stressed these cultural concerns, as opposed to outlining the more technical aspects of the study, consultants expressed a willingness to cooperate that can be attributed, at least in part, to their personal awareness of black oral history. It was in this context that I would mention why tape recordings are best suited to the task. At the same time, emphasis was placed on the value of as much firsthand contact with consultants as possible. The consultants were selected randomly through social networks, but I stressed the need to meet blacks who had strong views about the role of black people in American society and who, by extension, felt that they could express these issues in terms of their own experiences. I took care to indicate that I was not interested in interviewing just anyone; rather, as would be expected in the black vernacular culture, I expressed an open desire to talk to people especially tuned to the black American cultural experience.

Upon establishing this goal—to record experienced members of the community—I was then prepared to make the final arrangements for scheduling interviews. Whenever possible I would end preliminary interviews by making arrangements to continue at another time and, perhaps, at another location. This was usually agreeable, and by the fourth year of the Los Angeles study some consultants had come to expect their annual series of interviews. Throughout the years I have been fortunate to have met individuals who expressed a willingness to discuss the roles of blacks in America in a variety of social settings or to discuss such matters with others—both black and white—whom they were meeting for the first time. The linguistic adaptations outlined in chapter 5 have resulted, to a very large degree, from the social relationships among participants during the various interviews.[2]

There are, nevertheless, potential problems with the procedure that I employed, because of the uncommon nature of requests to record oral histories. Students of natural conversation, regardless of where they are working, will ultimately have to grapple with the fact that personal relationships and the exchange of immediate perceptions during an interview can influence the reliability of the data. Different fieldworkers will experience varying degrees of success as they try to unobtrusively gather interviews that correspond closely to vernacular styles.

This observation should not imply that I somehow overcame all the barriers associated with the observer's paradox, because I did not. Many prospective consultants were openly hostile to the idea of being interviewed, while others seemed almost eager for the chance.

---

2. All interviews were recorded with a Sony TC-140 cassette recorder. A lavaliere microphone (ECM 16) was used for most of the single interviews, and the open condenser microphone was used during group recordings. Once a consultant had agreed to be recorded, it was a fairly simple matter to request that we conduct the interview in quiet surroundings. I explained that transcription of the tapes was nearly impossible if they contained background noises, like television and radio. Everyone whom I spoke with considered this to be a reasonable request and cooperated without hesitation.

By trying to meet as many people as possible through frequent contacts over time—not merely for linguistic interviews—I had access to social domains that provided a clearer picture of the ethnographic situation. As in other areas that suffer from poverty and race-related problems, residents were openly cautious. They placed a high priority on minding your own business.

The observer's paradox, then, expands when the goals of descriptive adequacy collide with vernacular norms that correspond to a local philosophy where people "keep their business off the street." Here we attempt to solve this problem through the interview format. All questions were designed to reinforce, as often as possible, the need for individual life histories as a basis for reconstructing Afro-American history and culture. For those blacks who believe their history to be an important matter—and most of the consultants whom I spoke with do—personal histories represent a legitimate vernacular topic. Through the careful procedure of interviewing the same people over consecutive summers, I was gradually accepted by some consultants, while others were recorded less regularly.

The data that were recorded in the latter years are far more authentic in terms of the street vernacular than was material acquired in preliminary interviews with the same speakers. While this general pattern holds true, it is equally significant to appreciate that, while some individuals warm to one another quickly, others are more hesitant. This reflects the natural diversity of human personalities and should not detract from the fundamental observation that gradual familiarization is likely to generate more trustworthy samples of adult vernacular speech.

At this point one might ponder the prospect of conducting interviews with close (black) friends or family. After all, if a general principle of familiarity and colloquial speech is the case, would it not be easier to collect the most natural conversations through our intimate acquaintances? In this study I have stayed away from interviewing friends and family. Preliminary interviews with friends seemed—at least in my case—to be quite contrived; since they knew that I already knew their answers to many of the interview questions, we only created awkward conversations due to our shared knowledge. Interviews are rare speech events, and few of us engage in them on a frequent or daily basis. All true interviews share one common trait: new information is exchanged when the person asking the question does not already know the other person's (that is, the consultant's) answer. When new acquaintances are made, just as when new friendships are made, the fieldworker can ask questions that result in a true exchange of new ideas. However, when extensive personal experiences are common, as between husbands and wives, the interview can become contrived because both parties have so many related experiences.

Once preliminary contacts had been established with new acquaintances and once the tape recorder was accepted as part of the contacts, potential friendships or confrontations could develop. The next logical step focused on how to collect natural conversations or, as Wolfson (1976) has observed, how to create a social climate where the appropriate speech for the interview mirrored the street speech of everyday life. This objective was handled by devising questions tailored to the cultural values of the consultants themselves, in this case members of the black street culture.

Labov (1972a, 1972b) and Wolfram and Fasold (1974) have outlined a series of questions that can be used in most sociolinguistic interviews, but I took a slightly different approach. All my preliminary interviews began with the following questions, which focus on the contributions of blacks to the development of American music. In every new interview, the questions were asked in the same sequence. Thus, there were some occasions when consultants had more than one opportunity to discuss their views on the same topics with different groups of people.

> J.: Do you feel that blacks have made an important contribution to the development of music in the United States?

This proved to be an excellent introductory question because all speakers, regardless of class, age, or education, agreed that blacks have made a significant contribution. Responses spanned a wide range of opinion, as would be expected, but this affirmative reaction was categorical. While the question could have been answered with a simple yes or no, everyone discussed the issue at great length.

Once the topic of musical contribution had been discussed, I would then ask about the potential importance of this topic for public school curricula. Without exception everyone stressed that this kind of historical information is essential for an adequate education, especially for black children. It was usually during the course of these remarks that appropriate personal questions were raised regarding each speaker's educational experience. The following question was always asked at some point:

> J.: Did they teach about black music at the time when you were growing up?

Another categorical response was recorded: no. Since I framed the preceding question in this manner, all consultants were given an opportunity to initiate comments about their personal experiences. Thus, by answering my questions about musical topics—always in the preceding order—speakers were able to discuss issues that were clearly related to black culture and directly relevant to their personal experiences.

This preliminary format inevitably led to a variety of more or less closely related topics. My primary concern was to see that the conversations flowed with regularity. As to direct influence on the corpus, some questions were carefully framed to elicit past, present, and future tenses. I would therefore take care to introduce a variety of topics concerned with historical events, their present consequences, and future implications.

For example, Leo (a pseudonym, as are all the consultants' names in this book) began to discuss some of his encounters with police as a young man. My questions on this topic concentrated on his youth, thereby provoking dialogue that was framed in the past tense; related questions were stated in terms of posterity in an effort to evoke future-tense marking. However, this manipulation of tenses, which is well suited to colloquial conversation, represents the only overt manipulation of linguistic behavior on my part.

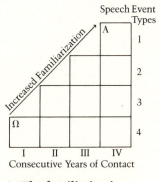

4. The familiarization process

Let us now consider the nature of the familiarization process. While the familiarity model is conceptually useful—see figure 4—it oversimplifies the true nature of varying familiarization processes. Two of the primary consultants illustrated this point as they came to use their vernacular styles with greater frequency, but at different rates.

David W. was very relaxed in the interview and therefore used his vernacular styles after a short period of time. This rapid familiarization is illustrated in figure 5. In the case of James D., however, the familiarization process took much more time. In fact, James eventually admitted that he was extremely suspicious of the tape recordings for at least a year; he simply did not see the point of the research. He considered any study that did not have immediate lifesaving applications to be a futile endeavor. Nevertheless, in later years, as illustrated in figure 6, James became more involved in different interview sessions and eventually conducted an interview in my absence.

Figures 5 and 6 represent a more realistic picture of the different rates for familiarization; however, with this flexibility in mind, the ideal model in figure 4 is most useful for reviewing the general familiarization process. Thus omega to alpha corresponds to increasing familiarity, and each of the speech event types will be discussed in terms of an ideal one-to-one ratio between consecutive years of contact and subsequent access to more familiar speaking domains. Each speech event category will be referred to by years of contact (roman numeral) and event type (arabic numeral), respectively.

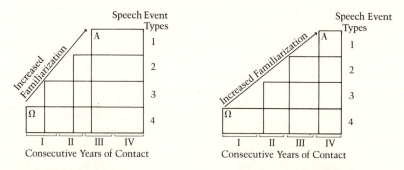

5. Rapid familiarization   **6. Delayed familiarization**

The most formal interviews (I-4) were of course recorded during the first year of contact. In the early stages of this study, informants often demonstrated high levels of formality in both their linguistic and their social behaviors. In some cases, like David's, my prior knowledge of a person would expedite familiarization. By the second summer (II-3), many people had become well acquainted with my practice of carrying a tape recorder for interviews. In II-3 speech events it is important to recall that consultants are well known to one another but that speech community membership is not a common factor. Type 3 interviews, while marked by vernacular dialogue, are not consistent with regard to the predominance of vernacular speaking styles. In these speech events we find a tendency toward formalization, in spite of the established familiarity.

There was more frequent use of the vernacular in the third summer of interviews (III-2), and it was during this summer, 1975, that I first resided in the area. I was thus able to have much more frequent contact with many residents from the neighborhood in a variety of public settings. It was clear during the third summer of recording that my presence was fairly well known to many residents. It was also during this third summer of fieldwork that I began to express my own opinions about topics with more personal freedom; that is, I no longer felt that it was appropriate or acceptable for me to maintain an implicitly neutral position in discussions on subjects I was responsible for initiating. It became more common for occasional arguments to occur. The most familiar interviews were recorded in the fourth year (IV-1), as would be expected.

Two anecdotes illustrate the value of ethnosensitive methods at all stages of fieldwork. One episode concerns JoJo and a group of his friends. They had at one time been employed as helpers at the pool, and, because the pool was a focal point of summer gatherings, former employees often visited the facility. At that time JoJo was nineteen and about to join the army. Like many men about to join the service, he decided to have one last night of civilian freedom before he was shipped to boot camp, so he partied hard. His final night of freedom, however, began at about 11:30 in the morning, and when I saw him it was almost 1:45 P.M. He was mildly intoxicated, but his demeanor was very friendly. It was, in fact, in this spirit of friendship that he offered a swig of a homemade brew consisting of a mixture of a hearty wine and a stout malt liquor. I blurted out a quick rejection upon hearing the contents of the concoction, "Man, I don't want none of that shit." To which JoJo responded with an equally quick retort, "Oh . . . you must be too good to drink my brew, huh?"

> J.: I'm not sayin that . . . I'm just sayin I don't want none. [Smiling, in an effort to defuse the situation.]
> JOJO: [Raising his voice] Well . . . hold on then, motherfucker . . . y' know . . . cause some people just ain't born with no silver spoon in they mouth . . . like you! [Group begins to laugh.]

At this juncture it is critical to appreciate that JoJo, at nineteen, was not legally allowed to buy liquor—he usually had to drink what was available. My rejection of his well-intended offer was therefore perceived as a personal rejection, although my initial comment was not intended as a put-down. His comment about the silver spoon was a direct attack on my status as a college man (that is, a prospective know-it-all). My immediate response was therefore especially important because it set the stage for my future interactions with all witnesses to the episode:

> J.: Hey my man, I'm not nobody that knows nothing about no silver spoon . . . but . . . I ain't gon drink no jet fuel . . . if

you want to kill yourself . . . tha's your business . . . I got
nothing to do with it.

JOJO: Shit . . . you just gettin old . . . can't take your drink no
more.

J.: Well . . . I guess you're right, young blood . . . the way you
been drinking . . . you must be right.

At that point JoJo quickly thrust his head back and drank the remaining contents of the container. When he finished, he raised his
arms and, turning slowly, smiled at everyone and said, "Now nobody's got to worry about if they like it or not . . . cause it's gone
now."

In situations like the preceding, personal hostilities can easily
flare up if slight misreadings of events are not quickly appeased.
Without some prior awareness of the ethnographic context, the
fieldworker may find that irreparable harm can befall promising relationships. In retrospect I must admit that I would like to have
handled the situation differently, but spontaneous reactions are another aspect of the observer's paradox that cannot be discounted.

The next illustration serves to reinforce the fact that ethnosensitivity is essential at all stages of the investigation. On the day in
question, I had scheduled an evening interview with Ted H. and his
wife. He told me to pick up a six-pack of beer and meet him at his
apartment. When I arrived I was met by his wife, Gail, who introduced herself and put some beer in the refrigerator. She then excused
herself, explaining that she had to fold clothes in the bedroom. She
also told me that Ted was taking a shower and would be with me
shortly. After a moment she came back and turned on the stereo. I
offered her a beer as she passed through the room; she then turned
back to the refrigerator and brought me a can of beer as well. As she
walked back to the bedroom, she told me to feel free to change the
volume on the stereo. I began to check my recording equipment in-
stead, making sure that everything was functioning. As I was testing
the voice level on the microphone, someone placed a key in the
front door. At first I was startled, but I assumed that anyone with a
key would surely be welcome. A young woman entered and introduced herself as Gail. I did a double take, and before I could really
say anything she continued, saying, "Y' know . . . Ted's wife; who
are you?"

I was not sure what was really happening, but my immediate
response was to avoid any family conflict. I introduced myself, men-
tioning the pool and my interviews with Ted. The new Gail looked
at me with some surprise and inquired further:

G.: Well, what are you doing here?

J.: I'm supposed to interview Ted now.

G.: Where is he?

J.: [Points to the bedroom without speaking.]

By now I was feeling quite uncomfortable, because I had not expected to meet *two* wives. The second Gail continued with more questions:

G.: How come Ted didn't tell me nothing about it?

J.: I don't know . . . maybe he didn't think about it.

G.: What's he doing? [Glancing around the room] . . . where is he?

J.: I think he's taking a shower.

G.: Naw . . . you can hear the shower when it's on.

It was at this point that I too realized that I had not really heard any water running in the small apartment.

G.: Why you think he took a shower?

J.: [Shaking head from side to side slowly and shrugging in confusion.]

G.: Did you bring him home from work? I didn't see his car.

J.: No, I don't know how he got home . . . why don't you go in there and see what he's doing? [Pointing again to the bedroom.]

G.: [Raising her voice] How did you get in here?

I truly did not know what to say now, because it was the other Gail, not Ted, who had let me into the apartment in the first place. However, the second Gail began to smile after she asked me about my presence, and eventually the smile grew until she broke into open laughter. As she continued to laugh, beginning to hold her sides, she walked over to the bedroom and told Ted and the first Gail to come into the living room. In actuality the second Gail was Ted's sister-in-law and the first Gail was truly his wife. This conspiratorial hoax was largely staged to test me; the full intentions of the ploy, however, still escape me.

Each of the preceding illustrations demonstrates the critical importance of ethnosensitivity in research of this kind. Every fieldworker will of course experience a variety of new situations that will require spontaneous action. These remarks are therefore not intended to address the multiplicity of circumstances that fieldworkers are likely to encounter; rather, by stressing ethnosensitivity we come to address two major goals essential to the present methodology:

1. As indicated earlier, the linguistic analyses require that every

consultant be interviewed in a variety of situations—in this case, the four specified speech event types.

2. Only those blacks who primarily interact with other black street speakers are considered to be the most representative consultants for an examination of black street speech.

As mentioned repeatedly, these goals take time, and the time that is required seems to vary directly with each consultant's personal ease in different interview settings.[3]

We have now come full circle regarding data collection, but many new questions stand before us. Thus far I have tried to demonstrate that two major hurdles affect studies of black street speech. First, we need a clear perception of grammatical boundaries; second, we must gain gradual access to the data through the eventual cooperation of street speakers themselves. We nevertheless return to the role of linguistic science in this enterprise, because a complete account of the facts can easily be distorted by theoretical preconceptions. My objective here is traditionally descriptive; I hope to account for the nature of black street speech as it breathes to accommodate existence in black and white societies. The major philosophical point that must be made, however, takes us back to Chomsky's dismissal of the theoretical significance of descriptive linguistics: "We have here good descriptive linguistics, but it takes no sophistication in linguistics to establish the socially relevant conclusion" (1977:55).

Based on the evidence that I have collected, where the same adults exhibit noticeable adjustments in their linguistic behavior in various situations, there is a need to examine aspects of linguistic behavior that are beneath thresholds of conscious awareness. In other words, when consultants have been told that their dialect is incorrect, they interpret this as meaning that their speech is ungrammatical. Yet as linguists view grammaticality these street

3. The overall corpus consists of over two hundred hours of recordings: forty-nine of these hours comprise data from nine primary adult informants; the other hours represent a supplementary corpus from other adult speakers who were interviewed in some, but not all, of the four speech event types. Each recording has been transcribed in three or four stages. The first transcription concentrated on all /-s/ variables, that is, contracted *is*, plurals, possessive marking, and third-person singular /-s/. The second series of transcriptions examined postvocalic and intervocalic /r/ and *are*, along with past-tense consonant cluster simplification. Pertinent syntactic constructions, various lexical items, and other examples of consonant cluster simplification were recorded during the third and fourth series. Some syntactic and lexical evidence was also recorded in writing when relevant utterances were spoken in other social settings.

speakers are simply using another dialect—a very distinct dialect—of English. Few of us who are native English speakers can examine the precise boundaries between standard and nonstandard dialects introspectively. It is just for this reason that I believe Chomsky underestimates the theoretical potential of descriptive linguistics. The procedures that have been used here are well known and have their origin in the earliest studies of Boas and Sapir. As such I am not advocating that we devise a new science to study minority populations; rather, we should make every effort to use the best available methods to meet the special problems involved in studying oppressed groups.

I have chosen linguistics for descriptive accuracy, and here I again part company with Chomsky. Some dimensions of linguistic behavior, the typical conversations that ordinary people use as part of their day-to-day existence, change in a systematic way without conscious monitoring. People tend to know when they are being formal, but they are not *fully* aware of every nuance of these changes. It is at this level, where people make slight subconscious adjustments, that inductive linguistics is at its best. As is the case for nearly every branch of science, linguistics has an inductive and a deductive tradition. In physics, chemistry, and the social sciences we still find productive contributions from both camps. My position is a simple one: considering the actual nature of conversation, a strict linguistic study offers a level of precise description and analysis that is not afforded by the study of other human behaviors. In chapter 5 we attack the problem head-on; having taken the time to collect the data, how can we analyze the facts to describe black street speech?

5
Specialized Lexical Marking and Alternation

The distinction between conscious and subconscious linguistic behavior is not always clear. Taboo words represent a good example of the kind of conscious control that we all maintain in monitoring our speech. The same holds true for aspects of black street speech. Language, when viewed in real-world contexts, has flexibility. This flexibility is rather complex, and no one has complete control over every linguistic nuance during ordinary conversation. Talking can take place under so many circumstances that we all too often take speech for granted. This is especially true when language attitudes and group loyalties are reflected by dialect usage. Our Cockney example serves, once again, to illustrate the case.

Some people learn Cockney as their native dialect, only to learn and use received pronunciation as a second (adult) dialect. Others, for one reason or another, may not learn the standard speech pattern, due to either personal choice or limited exposure. Most people are aware of stylistic alternation in speech and recognize the need for linguistic elasticity. Confidential conversations, for example, are often marked by circumstantial factors that are seldom verbalized. In spite of this awareness, we still do not overtly control all aspects of our speech. Most English speakers will pronounce the suffix -ing in two ways, namely, -ing / iŋ/ or /Iŋ/ and -in /In/. It is therefore possible that the same speaker could produce sentences with identical syntax and vocabulary but with alternate pronunciations. "Are you going?" versus "Are you goin?" should not raise any eyebrows during a conversation. However, when such subtle (for example, phonological) differences become associated with a particular group, they tend to adopt the relative prestige or stigma attributed to that group. Some accents are held in high esteem while others, like Cockney, are not; this is another social fact that confronts various speakers in their day-to-day lives. The problems associated with negative reactions have also been major for many black street speakers. It is very difficult for these speakers to know exactly what it is about their

English, calling them sissies and exerting other forms of
ssure or exclusion. While these boys usually did better in
hoolwork, they were outcasts on the playground. This peer
e came to be a critical factor for many young men and
, because the mainstream (adult) society tends to reward the
eech that black teens reject during the highly formulative
cent years.

any black students who recognize the competitive nature of
can life find they need new tools for interacting. The major
ments that subsequently take place can easily fluctuate over a
range of behavior, and attitudes toward black and white di-
s can be quite diversified. When contacts with whites are lim-
proficiency in standard English varies. Several other factors
e into play as well; speaking with elders or discussing topics of
personal esteem can result in changes of linguistic style. Again,
type of behavior is not new to linguistic research. Blom and
mperz (1972) have discussed very similar processes among rural
akers in Norway. The task at hand is to examine the situation for
ck street speech.

Because certain black American speech acts have received so
uch attention from scholars, I will not be focusing on slang, the
zens, or signifying. Most black people are keenly aware of these
rbal rituals. On the other hand, very few people understand the
ariable nature of speech, although they are conscious that changes
re taking place. All too often nonstandard speakers hold them-
elves responsible for not being able to produce standard English,
even though the historical facts are stacked against them. Through a
combination of quantitative and qualitative procedures, we can now
look at street speech in microscopic detail. By comparing the speech
of the same individuals in a variety of social contexts, we come to
learn how street speech breathes.

Technical analyses of linguistic behavior are nevertheless quite
limited, in spite of the detailed analytic accuracy they afford. A
speaker's frame of mind is still beyond our descriptive grasp, and ultimately most decisions are made as each utterance is formulated in
the mind. But by describing the end product, namely, the street
speech that is produced, we can detect stylistic shifts. Our more
complete picture of street speech shatters the early impressions fostered by Bereiter and Engelmann (1966) that it is a deficient linguistic system. There are limitations affecting street speakers, but they
are social and have no basis in linguistic fact. The impression that
street speech is inferior evolves from a combination of folk etymol-

speech that triggers negative response
experience, I know that most teache
aware of the nature of street speech;
given a distorted image of their dialect

In chapter 4 I mentioned that man
taught that their dialect is ungrammatic
throughout much of the educated An
blacks consider this serious enough that t
ers, linguists, therapists, and even drama c
sure from within and outside the vernacu.
tempts have been made to eradicate, suppl
speech with standard English. Most approac
reason or another, and, to the best of my kno
nique has proved successful on a large scale. T
of nonstandard English go far beyond linguisti
complete picture of street speech is needed bef
tional policy can be formulated. Here we concel
tic dimensions: what changes take place when :
toward standard English or vice versa?

In spite of my objective of looking at this proc
this survey is not comprehensive. Intonation, stre
sodic features have not been analyzed, although
tionably part of the style-shifting process. I have c
concentrate on those aspects of language that lingt
best equipped to describe: lexical variation, uniqu
usage, and phonological variation will receive the m
attention. Before we proceed, however, the general n
shifting should be considered.

Several well-known linguistic studies, including th
son (1959) and Brown and Gilman (1960), have demon
speakers control various components of language depen
speaking circumstances and/or whom is being talked t
cultures, for example, the type of language used in religiou
differs from that found in local taverns. We all recognize
and make the necessary (spontaneous) adjustments with
much difficulty; when an individual has problems with this
tic task, the likelihood of social problems can increase. Mc
depending on the linguistic experience of an individual, the re
adjustments may be more or less difficult. This issue is even
complicated for street speakers both because of the questic
group loyalty from within and because of social and economic
sures from without the vernacular black community. I remen
several occasions as a child when we would tease boys who sp

ogy and ethnocentric pronouncements. My account of this phenomenon provides a more complete survey of the subject.

In order to appreciate the full methodological problem at hand,
we can consider two related examples from western culture. The tradition of wearing neckties and high heels serves my purpose. Let us
assume for the moment that we are interested in knowing, as pre-
cisely as possible, when men wear ties and women wear high heels.
We could, in the Chomskyan tradition, engage in a series of thought
experiments to develop a theoretical model, predicting where and
when neckties and high heels are appropriate. As a first approximation, this might be a good idea—as it has been for linguistic science.
The actual answer, however, lies in the real-world (cumulative) behavior of men and women in day-to-day life. Our theoretical model
can take us only so far. Gathering data for this hypothetical study
would be a very sticky matter as well; not only would it be tedious,
but the fieldworkers would need to gain access to those situations
where the ties and the high heels were actually slipped on and off.
Needless to say, these are typically very private circumstances.

One might wonder—with some justification—how the study of
ties and high heels is connected with research on street speech. A
major similarity lies in the diversity of behavior that is adopted, as
well as in the need for a careful fieldwork strategy to collect the evidence without distorting the usual norms. Ties, high heels, and
street speech have their public and private faces, and if we have no
access to familiar surroundings any intimate behavior will be beyond our analytic grasp. At one extreme we find men who usually
wear ties, even in their homes, although this is a dwindling population. At the other end of the spectrum there are men who seldom, if
ever, wear ties. The same holds true for women and high heels; some
wear them always—including high heel slippers—while others
would never wear them. The real norm lies somewhere between the
extremes and defies simplistic categorization.

The study of street speech exhibits some striking parallels.
There are people who speak standard English exclusively, even in
vernacular contexts, while others use street speech regardless of the
situation. Once again the actual norm falls somewhere between the
opposite poles. All these examples point to a common fact. Norms
are shaped by the collective responses of individuals who exhibit
similar behavior under similar circumstances. Cultural norms, like
linguistic behavior, are not idiomatic phenomena. There must be
sources of social cohesion in order for communication and the advancement of civilization. For black Americans the task has been

one of survival. This social reality throws a different light on the linguistic situation.

Isolation from the mainstream has resulted in different paths of social evolution for black Americans. This also means that the corresponding linguistic evolution differs from that of other American minorities. In much the same manner that certain trees survive in the tortured climate above the timberline, black street speech survives below the poverty line as a relic of social inequality. It is not my intention to expound political or social philosophy here; I don't have the proper credentials or the desire to pursue the matter fully. However, there can be no question that the institution of slavery will continue to leave tremendous gaps between blacks and whites as long as the majority of blacks cannot compete with their white counterparts in the American job market. The linguistic dimension forms just a small segment of this picture, but it is the one dimension where social science can provide accurate insights. Again, it is primarily because of the exactitude of linguistic description that I have limited my study to this field.

In the remainder of this chapter, we will examine lexical variation in street speech. It will first be useful to specify certain terminology, namely, the distinction between code switching and style shifting. Other influential factors, such as topic-related variation, also serve to demonstrate the elastic nature of street speech.

Code Switching versus Style Shifting

Several influential linguistic studies have referred to code switching in black English, as well as in other bidialectal communities. In my opinion this stretches the terminology too far, especially for black street speech. Code switching has typically been used to refer to true bilingual situations, as with Spanish and English in the United States. Style shifting is not a bilingual process; the linguistic adjustments take place among intelligible dialects of a single language. Haugen (1964) emphatically made this distinction when certain linguists called for teaching standard English as a "foreign language" to black English speakers. He pointed out that bidialectalism was extremely difficult to master because of minor linguistic differences— that is, because standard English and nonstandard street speech are quite similar, it is very difficult to master the standard as a second dialect of the native vernacular. The task also seems to get more difficult with age.

In order to maintain this critical distinction, I will refer to street speech alternations as linguistic style shifts, which do not cross language boundaries. The term "code switching," on the other hand, should be reserved for truly bilingual cases, where at least two languages must be shared by the interlocutors.[1] This interpretation is still too cut-and-dried to match the actual diversity of stylistic options, but it is conceptually useful as a comparative model.

The bidialectal nature of street speech takes place on several linguistic levels simultaneously. In the remainder of this chapter we will survey four levels of lexical variation: topic-related shifting, syllable contraction and expansion, forestressing of bisyllabic words, and hypercorrection. The lexical evidence has been derived from two main sources: examples from the tape-recorded interviews and handwritten phonetic transcriptions that were immediately produced at the time of the utterance, that is, in addition to the recorded interviews. The contrastive examples compare tape recordings, transcriptions, and situations for the same consultants over a period of several years. It is this temporal dimension that distinguishes this work from most others on the same subject.

Topic-Related Shifting

I first became aware of the potential importance of topical influences for style shifting when listening to interviews recorded by John Lewis as part of Labov's detailed research (1972a) on black English in Harlem. Lewis, being black and personally familiar with his consultants, occasionally engaged them in detailed philosophical discussions. Those unfamiliar with street speech might have considered these to be heated arguments, but they were typical of vernacular conversational styles where positions are stated emphatically through expressive raising of the voice (see Kochman 1979, 1981).

In some instances, Lewis' consultants talked about topics touch-

---

1. My characterization of bilingual versus bidialectal phenomena implies a clear distinction between the two. Such an impression is wrong, although it serves my present purpose. From a purely linguistic point of view, the boundary between these processes is far more complicated. Weinreich (1953:18–47) has looked at this question in thorough detail and, to my knowledge, states the case most accurately. Namely, the actual distinction is a matter of degree. Contact vernaculars cannot be determined beforehand, and both linguistic and social factors come into play in determining the final linguistic product. Therefore the nature of each contact, as well as the attitudes of speakers toward one another, will ultimately determine the extent to which a particular language or dialect is learned and used.

ing their personal esteem. Debates raged over a wide range of social topics—for example, there were long discussions about the advantages and disadvantages of eating meat. When emotions ran especially high some consultants resorted to more standardized speech, while others made deeper shifts into the vernacular; these shifts in style initially appeared to be a personal matter. The same topic-related shifts that I observed in the Harlem data were occasionally present among my consultants. When topics of great personal importance were raised during the flow of conversation, some speakers would shift toward standard English while others would not.

As ethnographers of speaking have repeatedly observed, topics of discussion can indeed influence ways of speaking in different circumstances. From a theoretical standpoint, however, it is one thing to observe that particular topics are exerting special influences in a specific context; it is quite another to provide a formal definition of linguistic topics, including how they overlap and when they change.[2] The point at hand is a comparatively simple one: style shifts may be influenced to a greater or lesser degree by the speaker's personal assessment of the topic under discussion, although the same topic may trigger opposite style shifts from various street speakers.

Syllable Contraction and Expansion

Like many other American English dialects, street speech occasionally demonstrates a range of formal to informal pronunciations for the same word. In this case the phenomenon is not unique to blacks. Nevertheless, because street speakers vary their pronunciations in different situations, syllable alternation is quite pertinent to a complete appraisal of style shifting. The more informal the speaking circumstances, the more likely it is that words will be pronounced in the vernacular. In more formal settings some pronunciations mirror their standard English counterparts in the sense that they have identical syllable structures, but the characteristics of black English phonology are typically retained. This similarity among the syllables is more difficult to detect in contrast to standard English because they are nearly identical in form. Some of these variations are presented below in phonetic transcription:

2. Several problems emerge when a formal definition of topics is considered for linguists. Perhaps the most difficult aspect of a legitimate definition would be to identify explicitly the junctural and overlapping nature of topics as they shift, merge, and change capriciously in natural conversations.

Word	Very Formal	Formal	Informal
suppose		/səpoz/	/spoz/, /pozdə/
			(supposed to)
probably	/prabəli/	/prabli/	/prabli/, /prali/
because		/bɪkāwz/, /bikāwz/	/kāwz/
regular	/rɛgyəlɹ/	/rɛglɹ/	/rɛglɹ/, /rɛglə/
except		/ɛksɛp(t)/	/sɛpt/, /sɛp/

Illustrative formal and very formal sentences are as follows:

> . . . /səpoz/ you find that you can't help.
> That's not your job . . . you not /səpoz/ to put your hands on these kids at all . . .
> They /prabli/ changed the schedule.
> But—you see—most whites /prabəli/ don't understand the problem [stated to a white listener].
> That's /bɪkāwz/ you can't control it.
> . . . it's not /bikāwz/ they're stupid . . .
> The /rɛglɹ/ swimming lessons last two weeks.
> He don't keep /rɛgyəlɹ/ hours like everybody else.
> The office is open /ɛksɛp/ on the weekends.
> We closed everything /ɛksɛpt/ one window . . . and that's where they came in.

Illustrative informal sentences are presented below:

> If he /spoz/ to work for him, then I don't got nothing to say about it.
> How I'm /spoz/ to know what he wants?
> . . . you the one that's /pozdə/ deal with that . . .
> He /prabli/ went to the store.
> They /prali/ left by now . . .
> They jus kep on pushin /kāwz/ they knew he would back off.
> Well . . . I think . . . my /rɛglə/ schedule is on the bulletin board.
> They pay twenty-five cent, /sɛpt/ in the mornin . . .
> He would've finished school, /sɛp/ they kicked him out first.
> She would've won /sɛp/ for that bad start [referring to a track competition].

One of the more obvious reasons why many of these examples have not been singled out in the black English literature is that they are common to most English dialects. Speech tempo is also important, where rapid speech—which is more common in colloquial settings—produces the reduced syllables. Thus, when street pronunciations come to parallel those of standard English, they no longer stand out as clear points of contrast. But, because more data on the pronunciation of the same words in informal surroundings are now available, it is possible to identify the variable nature of some standardized pronunciations in greater detail, as illustrated by the preceding examples.

Each of the contrastive examples indicates that speakers reduce syllables quite regularly in the vernacular, especially when compared to their standardized pronunciation of the same words. This should not be surprising, because the process is not exclusive to blacks. Such variation, which operates at the level of complete lexical items, corresponds directly to the social situation where the word is used, and this is closely associated with what Hymes (1974) defines as communicative competence—that is, a speaker's ability to judge the immediate appropriateness of different linguistic styles. Without going into a detailed comparison of the psychological complexities of linguistic and/or communicative competence here, it can be said that the preceding variations demonstrate a very critical dimension of street speech style shifting, one that has not received a great deal of attention in the literature. Methodological restrictions are largely responsible for this gap in the evidence, because the relevant data are often sparse and appear rather sporadically. Research that relies on single interviews may not exhibit a full display of a consultant's available styles. More data will undoubtedly be required before definitive descriptions can be presented with any degree of reliability. In the meantime, the preceding examples point to a significant aspect of style shifting that relates to more complex psychological issues, such as those regarding the cognitive autonomy of a purely linguistic competence.

Variable Forestressing of Bisyllabic Words

Linguists have long been aware that blacks often use stress in ways that differ considerably from those of standard English speakers (see Rickford 1975). The following observations therefore add little to our present knowledge of street speech per se; rather, this information is primarily valuable in demonstrating that adults also use vernacular stress patterns in their colloquial speaking styles.

Nonstandard stress differences appear to vary in direct accordance with differing speech events, and they therefore reflect situational variation. While some variation can be observed in each of the speech event types, this alternation is weighted, with standardized stress patterns being favored in formal situations and vernacular patterns occurring more frequently—albeit for occasional stylistic effect—in less formal circumstances. The data that support this position, however, are comparatively sparse, and any situational correlations should therefore be thought of as tentative at this time.

To reflect momentarily on the diachronic implications of this type of syllable forestressing, some evidence from dialectology reveals that white Southerners in the United States employed similar forestressing patterns at one time. The more complicated task, one that will require more in-depth study, will be to establish the extent to which such phonological processes have been transferred between regional and ethnic groups in the United States and/or the extent to which internal linguistic factors affect corresponding usage. In the following sentences selected from adult street consultants, the primary syllable is stressed in each instance:

> If the pólice catch em, then he'll be sorry.
> But that's cause you let the man défine your problem.
> They can't lock . . . you they . . . they better próduce some evidence first.
> He say he ain't coming back to work less they révise the schedule.
> Well you know they gon détain a brother—just on principle.
> He gots to be pólite around his moms—an like it too.

This forestressing process—which is limited to a portion of bisyllabic words—is rather simple, as presented below (C = consonant, V = vowel):

Standard English   Black Street Speech
CV/CV́C   ⟶   CV́/CVC

Regardless of the fact that similar forestressing has occurred within other ethnic dialects in the United States, the present data indicate that the process is still active among adult street speakers. Street speech shows a general tendency to produce bisyllabic words with primary stress alternating variably between the first and the second syllables. In standard English, on the other hand, the corresponding examples are produced with primary stress on the second syllable.[3] Because this type of stress variation appears to be sensitive to speaking contexts, it would appear that adults have elevated this

---

3. While most standard English speakers say *próduce*, with primary stress on the first syllable, when referring to vegetables, secondary stress usually occurs when meanings are associated with aspects of production of some kind.

aspect of dialect difference to the level of (comparatively) conscious manipulation. In turn, some stress alternations would appear to be among the more apparent differences between standard English and the street vernacular because the variation affects entire lexical items.

Hypercorrection

The term "hypercorrection" has usually referred to any linguistic extension that exceeds the standard, becoming overgeneralized to a broader range of linguistic environments—for example, *pickted* /pɪktɪd/ or *giveded* /gɪvdɪd/. It will be useful to examine hypercorrection under two headings: reinterpretation and regularization of standard English paradigms. The examples where regularization takes place will prove to be the most interesting, because they expose the linguistic environments where standard English is most vulnerable to change in the future. In the specific instances of hypercorrection that were observed in the four speech event types, the general trend in formal speaking contexts resulted in most of the hypercorrect examples, but this was by no means categorical. The phonological variation presented in the examples below tends to occur in direct correspondence with the formality of the speaking situation. This being the case, there can be little doubt that hypercorrections embody some of the most perceptible dimensions of the style-shifting process. There are instances where hypercorrection seems to be somewhat random and not influenced by immediate speaking contexts, but there are other cases where situational correlations are much too regular to be coincidental.

Earlier studies of hypercorrection have concentrated on the prospective influence of internal linguistic constraints. For example, Labov and his colleagues observed that hypercorrect forms with *-ed* appeared randomly in the Harlem data: "Hypercorrection is typically an individual matter, and the sporadic and irregular character of its distribution reflects the fact that these forms are not controlled by any rule of *language*, in the sense of a grammar used by a speech community" (1968 : 152). While hypercorrections are random from the standpoint of internal linguistic patterning, social circumstances now appear to have a direct bearing on the hypercorrection process.

Reinterpretation   Reinterpretation typically occurs when street speech adds elements where standard English does not use the same form. A street speech sentence with "I likes . . ." could be considered a reinterpretation of the standard English paradigm. In a formal situation Ronald said, "They act like they think I really likes goin to school," while under more colloquial conditions, when talking about his new car, he produced the less stigmatized sentence, "I like the way it runs."

Additional examples reinforce the fact that reinterpretations are more likely to occur when speakers use their standardized variety, simply because it is under these conditions that they are less sure of "correct" usage. Pitts (1981) argues that some suffix /-s/ variation (that is, hypercorrection) is produced for stylistic effect.

Regularization   Other instances of hypercorrection commonly found in the corpus result from regularization of standard English paradigms. Such analogic extensions are well documented in the world's historical linguistic literature and need not be discussed at length here. The synchronic data reveal that excessive regularization is more likely to occur in formal contexts. Both Wolfram (1969) and Fasold (1972) have commented on the fact that hypercorrect /-s/ suffixes occur with greater frequency when standard usage is approached in discourse. In keeping with the practice of examining internal linguistic constraints, Wolfram accounted for hypercorrect suffix /-s/ usage among black working-class speakers and found that their use of pluralized /-s/ was based on analogic extensions of the predominantly standard English plural /-s/ rules.

Below, the data on hypercorrect and colloquial pronunciations reveal that two linguistic processes seem to be operating. With hypercorrect /-s/ there are two rules that result in forms like *listes* for *lists*; and the *-ed* morpheme is often reduplicated when speakers are confused about the location of morpheme boundaries in relevant clusters:

Predominant Formal Pronunciations	Predominant Informal Pronunciations
likes /layks/	like /layk/
lises /lɪsɪz/	lis(t) /lɪs/
teses /tɛsɪz/	tes(t) /tɛs/
two-faceded /tufeystɪd/	
lookted /lʊktɪd/	looked /lʊkt/
waxted /wækstɪd/	waxed /wækst/
loveded /lʌvdɪd/	loved /lʌvd/

With the second and third examples above, that is, with suffix /-s/, a two-step process accounts for these productions. First, there is the simple case of apocope that eliminates the final /-t/ in /-st/ clusters; thus in colloquial speech *list* becomes *lis*. Usually the discourse will establish the singularity or plurality of noun phrases in natural conversation, and street speakers have been able to use pronunciations like *lis* or *tes* without any real need to distinguish singulars from plurals; most discourse conveys this information. Second, in more formal contexts, where street speakers are—for whatever reason—attempting to introduce distinctions not part of their native vernacular, the regular standard rule for plural marking with /-s/ is adopted with greater frequency, thereby producing forms like *lises* and *teses* in formal speech.

The examples with *-ed* are affected by a different process, where the final consonants are appended with an additional syllable and suffix (that is, /ɪd/).

As in the preceding examples, the discourse context can play a major role in establishing the intended tense marking without direct reference to the presence of past-tense (that is, *-ed*) allomorphs, but speakers can easily confuse the nature of the final consonant cluster. As observed by Labov and his colleagues (1968:153), "Speakers are behaving as if the cluster is *-kt* and not *-k # d*" (that is, a morpheme boundary). The final three examples illustrate this confusion and indicate that speakers adopt analogic extensions for emphasizing past tense with *-ed*. Again, this reduplication is not completely random but is favored in more formal speaking circumstances.

Street speakers are, quite understandably, likely to produce hypercorrections in similar linguistic environments based on morphological analogies with standard English. These hypercorrections will vary considerably depending on the individual's degree of exposure to standard English. Street speakers are therefore prone to produce errors in standard English that correspond to their understanding—or lack thereof—of this second dialect.

There are additional linguistic reasons why street speakers may confuse the distribution of these standard morphemes, because their function is often unclear or redundant in everyday speech. To clarify this point, let us return to some grammatical considerations that could trigger the use of hypercorrect forms. In the cases of *loveded* and *two-faceded*, the morphological status of *-ed* is ambiguous, depending on the environment where the words are used. While it is possible to say "Tom is loved," where *loved* is a predicate adjective, "Tom was loved" marks the transition to past tense with the auxiliary alone (that is, *was*). The potential for confusing the function of *-ed* as a predicate adjective may therefore be handled through reduplication in an effort to specify the past-tense status of the verb (that is, *loveded*). A similar argument holds true for *two-faced*, simply because there is no isolated form *two-face* in English.

From the preceding observations, it appears that the true explanation for hypercorrect variation goes beyond the traditional descriptive bounds of purely linguistic constraints in several cases. And, although additional data are needed to corroborate this point, the examples suggest that, while street speakers tend to regularize standard rules in formal situations, this analogic regularization diminishes in colloquial settings where the vernacular is more commonly found.

Lexical Summary

The linguistic variation that has been described here falls under four general headings: topic-related shifting, syllable contraction and expansion, forestressing of bisyllabic words, and hypercorrection. Because of the random nature of these variables throughout the corpus, my observations are minimally relevant to the larger question of situationally related style shifts. Nevertheless, by identifying these instances of lexical difference, where structural contrast with the standard is readily apparent, it becomes possible to expose dimensions of the vernacular that are actively employed by adult street speakers. As more details become available, the stylistic implications for this kind of variation can be examined in more depth and with greater reliability. With caution in mind, then, I would like to suggest that hypercorrection and syllable variation are to some degree influenced directly by situational factors. Beyond the situational influences, though, certain topics—those held to be of personal importance to speakers—are also potentially instrumental in the choice of speaking style.

6
Unique Grammatical Usage

Several grammatical differences between street speech and standard English can be identified, especially when conversational data serve as a basis for comparison. For our purposes, it will be most useful to concentrate on the nature of syntactic structures and their related functions initially in synchronic terms. Having reviewed these contemporary forms, we will consider some of the historical implications of linguistic influence from Anglican and African sources.

As observed with the lexical variation discussed in the preceding chapter, it can be extremely difficult to establish the degree to which situational constraints have a direct effect on the presence or absence of particular nonstandard sentences. This is largely because equivalent semantic sentences are not always available in standard English. Since grammatical differences are the object of analysis, only those examples where there is clear semantic equivalence to the standard can serve as sources of direct comparison. The final analysis shows that autonomous black street syntax is more likely to appear in vernacular speaking contexts than in formal situations. So, while we cannot establish direct links between situations and the probable occurrence of a particular grammatical sequence, it is evident that vernacular styles are used with far greater frequency in familiar surroundings.

Some anecdotal evidence will help clarify the discourse contexts of particular examples. We will be concentrating on six grammatical aspects of street speech: *be, done, be done*, stressed *been*, multiple negation, and aspectual *steady*.

Locating Suitable Examples

Some of the most important research in black English has concentrated on differences in tense and aspect systems. Tense relates to time, whereas aspect is associated with the way actions and/or events are conducted. Based largely on earlier research, my work locates many of the same cases for the adult street speech population. For example, invariant *be* (that is, habitual or durative *be*) has been discussed at considerable length by Fasold (1969, 1972), Dillard (1972), Stewart (1969), Fickett (1970), Wolfram (1969), and Labov and his colleagues (1968), among others; the grammatical status of perfective *done* has likewise been analyzed in great detail.

With rare exceptions, most of these pioneering analyses have been based on usage by younger members of the speech community. The study at hand, however, reveals that adults are actively aware of these grammatical forms and employ them frequently in their colloquial conversations. Because these grammatical differences have been so important to educators, it will be helpful to see how they function in broader adult contexts. Like the examples in the preceding chapter, relevant cases have been derived from two sources: some instances have been recorded on tape, while others were transcribed by hand. With written transcriptions I have adhered to the practice of analyzing those constructions that were recorded immediately on the scene; all secondary (that is, recollected) cases have been discarded as unreliable.

Syntactic Constructions and Their Functions

The general format for the syntactic discussion will be somewhat similar from case to case. Initially the grammatical status of a particular word or construction will be identified, and this definition will be placed in the proper context using suitable examples from the data. When appropriate we will review some of the social implications associated with particular forms.

With the exception of *steady*, described here for the first time, I will be focusing on cases that are well documented in the existing literature. As any student of black English knows, several explanations—some of them competing—can usually be found for each of the relevant examples. Also, as noted previously, the earliest descriptions were heavily influenced by the most obvious linguistic differences between street speech and standard English. While this practice has been vital to exposing unique dimensions of street speech, it is equally important to remember that there are overwhelming similarities between the dialects, and these similarities make the goal of definitive grammatical description a very elusive one. This is especially true because of the contextual (that is, pragmatic) dependence of so many relevant semantic examples.

Because language constantly changes, accurate descriptions can be difficult to obtain. However, by appreciating the ever-changing nature of language, we develop a greater respect for the fluidity of the phenomenon as unpredictable events in the human arena provide us with descriptive puzzles that defy categorization through idealized deduction.

A primary concern here is to demonstrate that adults in the street community have the linguistic competence to use the vernacular dialect as well as aspects of standard English on other occasions. Several authors have claimed that adults in the street community have been influenced by standard English norms and that these influences are confirmed by a lack of vernacular usage. The data presented here differ from this position; in colloquial settings adults clearly have the option to use nonstandard speech, which is representative of the vernacular in its purest form. From the perspective of style shifting, however, there is no reliable way that a conversational corpus can adequately expose the equivalent standard alternative, if one exists. In the absence of data that can explicitly compare street speech and standard English, interdialect comparison is highly speculative at best. With this in mind, then, let us return to the nature of these unique grammatical functions.

Invariant *Be* Almost more than any other aspect of the vernacular, the use of *be* has been presented as one of the clearest examples of an autonomous dialect feature. Detailed accounts of *be*—and the alternative descriptions that correspond to these accounts—can be found in the writings of Stewart (1968b), Labov and his colleagues (1968), Fasold (1969, 1972), and Wolfram (1969), among others. All these scholars would agree that *be* represents a unique feature of street speech, but there is considerable disagreement regarding the linguistic functions that *be* fulfills.

Previous findings have shown clear habitual and/or durative functions typically associated with invariant *be*, as illustrated by the first two sentences below. Labov and Fasold have also observed two forms of *be* (that is, homonyms): one is similar in function to standard English, including *is*, *am*, and *are*; the other, the invariant distributive forms of *be*, is exclusive to street speech. Perhaps the most useful contribution that can be made here is to recognize that adults can use invariant *be* in much the same way as younger members of the speech community. Examples of adult use of invariant *be* are as follows:

When they get caught stealin—they *be* talkin bout how innocent everybody is.
She say, "Why you *be* runnin in the street so much?"

It's just not convenient . . . y' know . . . cause the office *be*
   closed on the weekends.
Them brothers *be* playin . . . they *be* blowin they souls out
   [referring to musicians].
But the teachers don't *be* knowing the problems like the parent do.
They just *be* doing they job . . .

These sentences are consistent with the functions that have already been described in other studies. At first blush this may not appear to be a significant point, but the historical transmission of *be* is
more readily understood when similar grammatical functions are active across generations of street speakers in the same area. Before reviewing historical alternatives, let us consider some of the grammatical accounts presented in the available literature to date.

Following Rickford, we will primarily concentrate on Fasold's
discussion of *be*, since it is the most detailed account of the form. As
noted previously, *be* can be used in ways that are similar to standard
English *am*, *is*, and *are*. Yet, in spite of these similarities, Fasold cau-
tions against the generalization of usage across dialects. Rickford
states the case as follows:

> The primary function of *be*, demonstrated with a wide vari-
> ety of evidence in Fasold (1972), is that of indicating habitual
> or iterative aspect. Fasold stresses the importance of distin-
> guishing occurrences of invariant *be* in this function, which he
> calls 'distributive,' from occurrences which are also found in
> standard English: *be* in imperatives (*Be* quiet!), subjunctives
> (If this *be* treason . . .), and after modal auxiliaries (can, may,
> should, etc.). It is particularly important to distinguish cases of
> habitual *be* from cases in which an underlying *will* or *would*
> has been deleted, but can be reconstructed from other evi-
> dence. (1974:97)

Rickford goes on to make the important observation that *be* is not
necessarily a semantically tenseless form, as Fasold indicates in his
original description. Rather, *be* occurs most frequently in habitual
contexts where events are nonpast or incomplete. The present findings support this position. Many of the sentences that occurred with
be were contextually related to incomplete events.

While Rickford's assessment receives additional support from
the present data, it would be unwise to suggest that habituality
alone should be considered the predominant characteristic for *be*. In
addition to these functions we find the somewhat similar durative

interpretations—that is, where an activity extends over a period of time but need not be of a habitual nature. Consider the following sentences:

> . . . and we *be* tired from the heat, but he just made everybody keep on working.
> So they *be* runnin . . . right . . . really bookin . . . and the police had all the streets blocked off.

In each of the preceding examples we find a durative reading, where the verb's action extends over a period of time. *Be* is also found with the historical present, perhaps varying with *was* in other environments.

To turn, then, to some of the pertinent historical implications, Rickford gathered data on contemporary Sea Island creole of South Carolina and constructed a strong case for the prospect that *be*, in some instances, may have developed as part of the nonpast referent of *doz* in Sea Island creole and in Guyanese creole. He also observes that there is an age-graded relationship with regard to the use of *be* in Sea Island creole in opposition to a more frequent use of *doz* and *doz be* by speakers over sixty. In short, *doz*, which is different from standard English *does*, is a habitual marker and as such is not truly part of the Sea Island creole auxiliary.

The value of Rickford's observations is most important here, because he has demonstrated that there are historical links between *doz be* and the evolutionary process which resulted in the isolated habitual marking of *be* for street speech. The reader is, of course, directed to Rickford's original discussion for more specific details; but, for contemporary adult usage of *be*, his work provides insights that have typically gone unnoticed because of the similar phonological and grammatical functions of Sea Island *doz* and standard English *does*. Spears (1982) observes a similar situation with *come* in street speech versus standard English.

To complete his historical orientation, Rickford also indicates that there is a great deal of evidence to suggest that Irish influences could easily have swayed the grammatical interpretation and evaluation of *be*. Traugott (1972a) has made similar observations in her book, *A History of English Syntax*. Looking at the nature of decreolization, Traugott stresses the need to focus our grammatical analyses on historical contexts from all known sources of contact, and as illustration she presents evidence about the migratory patterns of the Ulster-Scots who settled in the South as indentured servants. Eventually these individuals became the class of poor whites who, in their capacity as overseers, had extensive contact with slaves.

Thus, while there can be little doubt that decreolization was active in the Americas, if for no other reason than the absence of constant exposure to African languages, the question as to which English dialects served as models for black English is still subject to debate.

Once the true nature of social contact is considered in the historical sense, it is difficult to refute the fact that contemporary street speech has been influenced by a variety of sources. The folk speech of the Scots-Irish represents one of the most feasible sources of contact in decreolization. Traugott states the case as follows:

> The situation is remarkably similar to one that existed in many creoles, in which expression of aspect rather than tense is very important; but it is also similar to the situation in Old English and Middle English, with relics in Northern dialects [*sic*], when *beo-* and *wes-* were contrasted. Is this pure coincidence or can we postulate that the creole and English forms reinforced one another? The continuation of *I be* versus *I am* in Scottish dialects suggests that possibly *be* is not untypical of English as most investigators assume. (1972a: 191)

A full account of the historical situations—and, by extension, new insights regarding contemporary use of *be*—requires much more in the way of historical evidence from both the social and the linguistic perspectives. Nevertheless, based on the information that we have at this time, there appear to be aspectual functions associated with *be* that have dual origins. The historical interpretations, then, are unquestionably interconnected as far as the decreolization of slave-related dialects is concerned.

For style shifting it is extremely difficult to identify contrastive elements in standard English that represent suitable options to distributive *be* in the vernacular. *Be* usually occurs with much greater frequency in colloquial contexts where all speakers share the non-standard form. The following sentences illustrate typical adult usage:

—Verb+ing
He *be* hiding when he knows she's mad.
They *be* partying hard when Friday night rolls around.
. . . and those sisters *be* lookin so fine.

—Locative
They don't *be* on the streets no more.
If the police come, then they *be* in Pearce Apartments where nobody can find them.

—Noun Phrase
They *be* the real troublemakers.
Leo *be* the one to tell it like it is.
The Clovers *be* the baddest ones around here.

—Adjective
He *be* crazy when he's been drinkin.
It's not right—y' know—to act like you *be* stupid in school.

The preceding examples are nearly identical to many of the *be* occurrences that were recorded by Lewis in Harlem and by Wolfram in Detroit. Without question *be* is truly a national feature of street speech; furthermore, it is well known to adult street speakers.

Perfective *Done* The use of perfective *done* demonstrates many of the same descriptive problems that we have already encountered with the different uses and origins of *be*. That is to say, because of overlapping usage with white dialects—primarily southern white dialects—there are a number of historical alternatives that must be considered before an adequate evolutionary explanation can be tendered. Functionally speaking, we find that *done* is a perfective marker, and it is used with moderate regularity in colloquial contexts where suitable perfective comments are appropriate. Perfectives indicate completed actions. Sentences such as the following demonstrate that the use of *done* is rather similar, as Labov and his colleagues (1968) observed, to the use of perfective *have* and *already* in standard English, although this is not the complete function:

He *done* busted his lip.
The teacher *done* lost her keys.
He *done* left his trunks home.

The question of the relationship between perfective *have* and *already* and the corresponding meaning in street speech is undoubtedly complicated by alternative historical explanations, corresponding to the evolution and dissemination of these perfective grammatical functions, that is, as regards completed events or activities.

While it is possible to compare sentences in street speech and standard English, that is, where *done* is semantically similar in both, the derivation of *done* may have its origin in both African and Anglican sources. The fact that we can find more than one source of historic origin should not be surprising, considering the nature of the social contact in the Americas that brought blacks and whites with diverse languages together under the auspices of slavery. Dillard presents a case for *done* that rests primarily upon similar grammatical forms that can be found in the pidgins and creoles on the west coast of Africa. Examining the perfective aspect of *done* specifically, he states:

> Black English resembles West African languages grammatically in the Remote Perfective form and in a contrasting Immediate Perfective Aspect, for which the preverbal form is *done*. . . . Although Black English speakers, including relatively young speakers, do use the *have/has* auxiliaries at times, they use and manipulate them with a lack of skill which shows that they are really borrowing them from Standard English and not using the resources of their own language. The forms *been* and *done* come closest to the perfective function of *have* in Standard English . . . it is probably this resemblance which made it possible for southern white speakers to borrow *done* in structures like *have/has done gone.* (1972:47–48)

Feagin (1979) offers a different scenario for *done*, which traces nonstandard southern white usage to Anglican derivations. This, of course, suggests that the direction of borrowing is not so clear-cut, especially when similar data from older English-based dialects are compared directly with prior uses of *done*. Feagin's arguments are compelling and well researched. Based on her study, it seems more probable that white English speakers brought their own forms of *done* with them when they arrived in the United States, although these uses of *done* clearly contrast with standardized English in the Americas. The strongest evidence in support of this white influence has been discussed in detail by Wolfram and Christian in their analysis of Appalachian English, where perfective *done* is still used by older speakers in ways that are consistent with *done* usage in street speech.

Wolfram and Christian also provide the following definition for *done*, revising previous analysis of the form:

> . . . *done* is essentially "completive" in nature, referring to a characteristic of its meaning. Other proposals concerning the meaning of this form have been made and many simply suggest a close synonym, like the perfective auxiliary *have* or the adverb *already*. Although these both have aspects which show a similarity to *done*, neither is actually equivalent in meaning. (1976:87)

This position is reinforced by Feagin's research (1976) on white southern speech. As indicated by the preceding quote, the functions of *completely* and *already* are associated with meanings for *done*.

But these meanings do not entirely capture some of the examples from adult speakers. Although *done* appears to be a subsiding feature in the data, the illustrative sentences show that it has overlapping similarities with white usage. Some noteworthy distinctions are nevertheless relevant to the analysis at hand.

Before proceeding, a word of caution may be helpful. While it is true that several analyses of *done* can be found in the literature, most scholars have not generalized these findings to include both street speech and nonstandard white use of the form. It may still be too early to assume that *done* can be analyzed as a general feature of nonstandard American English dialects—that is, across class, geographic, and ethnic bounds. While Labov's analyses have properly been compared to their Appalachian counterparts, he makes no claim that his definitions should be extended to white dialects. Fasold and Wolfram, on the other hand, have presented their discussion of *done* in a way that includes most nonstandard varieties of English. This distinction is critical to understanding differences in various technical studies of this form.

Looking at the following sentences with *done*, recorded during my fieldwork, I can appreciate the desire to draw analytic parallels between black and white usage, but when the historical alternatives are weighed there are several good reasons for separating the utterances of black and white speakers. Examples of *done* used in casual conversation by adult street speakers are as follows:

> We *done* told him bout these pipes already.
> You *done* spent up all your money, that's why! [You're not getting any of mine.]
> They *done* sold all the Smokey Robinson tapes.
> I *done* forgot to turn off the stove.
> It don't make no difference, cause they *done* used all the good ones by now.
> Well, we useta get into trouble, and . . . y' know . . . like . . . if Pop'd catch us, he say, "Boy—you *done* done it now."

It is not altogether clear, based on the preceding examples, whether one should look to African-related sources, like those described by Dillard (1972), or whether more reliable answers can be found in older English forms, like those discussed by Hancock (1975), Feagin (1976), and Traugott (1972b). There is, of course, plenty of justification for considering a compromise that would account for the distinctions—and similarities—which may have originally been influenced by African sources. These African influences may have then been preserved in postslavery America due to racial isolation (that is, linguistic isolation).

As far as contemporary usage is concerned, two main functions should be considered with the preceding examples for *done*: perfective functions and an intensifier role similar to that of *really*. The first four sentences above also have a clear perfective status due to the completed nature of their events. The fifth sentence is one of the best examples for comparison with *already*, while the last sentence combines different grammatical functions for *done* to emphasize the perfective meaning.

The preceding examples are rather sparse within the corpus, but the following case proves to be very interesting from the standpoint of grammatical function. Some additional background will be useful to place the sentence in its proper context. Once, while I was preparing to interview two young women near the pool, I happened to see Diane M.; we greeted each other and she walked over to where I was preparing to record. She was visibly upset, and I asked her if anything was wrong. After some initial reluctance, she admitted that she and her husband were having marital problems. She began by speaking of their economic difficulties, but as she continued it became evident that her husband had been having an affair. Diane's husband worked the graveyard shift at a local factory, and she had tried to call him at work only to find that he had not reported for the evening. It was in this context that she said:

> So he went to where she was . . . and got the nerve to lie to me
> . . . talking bout he *done* went to work.

For the purpose of linguistic analysis, the status of *done* in this sentence is definitely not captured by *already* or *completely*. The intensifier function would appear to be best suited to the preceding example, but other interpretations may prove to be valid as more reliable samples are compared with data from other representative speakers. These observations are most useful here because they demonstrate that street speech and white Appalachian communities still use *done* in some shared ways.

Future Perfective *Be Done* *Be done* is primarily used as a future perfective in black street speech and occurs with past-tense verbs to fulfill this function. Based on the present evidence, it is reasonable to assume that this usage developed among black English speakers in the United States and perhaps among speakers of other English-derived creoles in the Americas. The form generally serves to mark predictions (that is, consequences or results) of events that will or perhaps can be completed at some time in the future.

For example, Labov does not discuss the following sentence in relation to the future orientation of the remark: "'Cause I'll be done put—stuck so many holes in him he'll wish he wouldna said it" (1972a: 56). The sentence clearly indicates that the event will be taking place at some point in the future. Similarly, a young couple from Los Angeles were arguing over which one of them would have enough money to buy a new car first, at some future date; the woman exclaimed, "I'll be done had my car by November." The perfective status is implied in this context because she expects to complete the action before November.

This construction appears relatively infrequently in the data, but the following sentences are representative, and in every case there is an unmistakable future orientation:

> We be done washed all the cars by the time JoJo gets back with
>   the cigarettes [said at a church-sponsored car wash].
> I'll be done bought my own CB waitin on him to buy me one.
> They be done spent my money before I even get a look at it.

A critical survey of these examples shows that the use of be done is not a simple merger between the meanings of either be or done, nor do we see any direct association with historical sources beyond the Americas. While future perfectives exist in many languages, the use of be done in this manner is perhaps the result of a blended substitution of words, that is, where proto-African words were preserved by the adoption of an English word to carry on the original grammatical function. Be done would be an instance of this kind of word substitution, or relexification, for a two-word construction that has been adopted by street speakers to expand the grammatical capacity of their own dialect. Regardless of its origin, be done usually predicts the completion of some future event. The broader nonpast usage typically occurs with verbs in the past-tense form, thereby reinforcing the perfective function.

If we use the first two sentences above as sources of comparison and manipulate the tense of the verb, the special functions for be done can be exposed. First the adoption of suffix /-s/ will produce ungrammatical sentences:[1]

> *We be done washes all the cars . . .
> *I'll be done buys my own CB . . .

---

1. An asterisk indicates that the corresponding sentence is ungrammatical.

The preceding examples are particularly interesting because street speakers interpreted the sentences as being composed of the isolated words *be* and *done*, as opposed to *be done* as a single grammatical construct. With this being the case the sentences were rejected because *done* is exclusive to the past tense, largely because it is a true perfective.

The situation is slightly more complicated when progressive verbs are substituted:

We *be done* washing all the cars . . .
I'll *be done* buying my own CB . . .

These sentences are not ungrammatical in the colloquial sense, but they suffer from the same confusion that influenced the interpretations of the ungrammatical sentences above; namely, several street speakers considered *be* and *done* as separate words, where *done* was semantically equivalent to *finished*:

We *be finished* washing all the cars . . .
I'll *be finished* buying my own CB . . .

While these sentences are grammatical, they do not correspond to the speakers' original meaning when they used *be done* as a non-past form. Another possibility, more in line with the original intentions of the speakers, can be expressed by a general rule—presented below—of consequential or resultative implications for *be done*, where NP__ . . . is a noun phrase, excluding sentences with a sentence-initial indefinite article (for example, "*A girl be done sang"):

NP__ *be done* (X) before (Y). → (X) then (Y) as a result.

Each of the first three sentences applies to this rule, as illustrated below:

We *be done* (washed all the cars) /by the time/ (JoJo gets . . .).
I'll *be done* (bought my own CB) /waitin on/ (him to . . .).
They *be done* (spent my money) /before/ (I even . . .).

In each instance, (X) represents an event that takes place and is completed before (Y), that is, the agent, completes the action or process.

While this rule holds true for the preceding examples, there is an isolated example where it does not apply. One day at the pool, there was an incident between a white lifeguard and a black male teenager. The boy had been taunting the guard with repeated racial insults, which the guard ignored. Eventually the insults amplified to a rapid escalation of events where the teenager spat on the guard and, as he tried to retreat, was thrown by another (black) lifeguard into the pool. At that point the white guard jumped into the pool and dunked the teenager repeatedly; by the time the episode was over both parties were exhausted. Everyone thought the conflict had ended, but later that evening the boy's father returned to the pool to "knock that motherfucking honky upside his head." Fortunately, the black guards were able to prevent any physical violence, but tempers flared and in the heat of anger the young man's father said:

> I'll *be done* killed that motherfucker if he tries to lay a hand
> on my kid again!

The formulated rule does not apply in this case but is replaced by a slightly modified version:

> NP__ *be done* (X) if (Y). → (Y) then (X) as a result.

Stated briefly, the sequence of the events is changed, although both statements have predictive focuses. In this instance there is an unquestionable perfective implication because the guard is not dead (killed) at the moment of speaking; rather, he will be killed only in the event that he completes (Y), the act of laying hands on the child again. While this is the only example of its kind in the corpus, the circumstances emphasize the grammatical diversity of *be done* as well as the unique status of this usage in street speech.

Stressed *Been*   John Rickford (1975) is most responsible for bringing stressed *been* to the attention of linguists and other scholars. While many have observed *been* before, Rickford's research is the first to examine the vernacular autonomy of the stressed form. Close examination of the linguistic environments where *been* appears and of the unique meanings that correspond to it has been responsible for revealing grammatical functions that had previously gone unnoticed.

There were several occasions when adults used *been* in ways that are consistent with Rickford's observations. All the sentences where *been* was used by adults appear below and refer to stressed forms of the word:

> We *been* lived here.
> She *been* told him she needed the money.
> I *been* had that job.
> I *been* had that car.
> They *been* called the cops, and they're still not here.
> I *been* cleaned the stove.

He *been* had that scar.
They *been* fixed the door.
He *been* been in jail.
I *been* been knowing Russell.

Some additional background may be helpful. In earlier studies of *been*, most scholars observed that perfective meanings were usually attached to the word; moreover, these perfective functions were always found in contexts with progressive verbs (see Stewart 1967; Fickett 1970; Fasold and Wolfram 1970; Dillard 1972). As Rickford observed, however, the unique functions of *been* can occur with stative verbs as well (that is, verbs which indicate states as opposed to actions). He captures the range of pertinent meanings as follows:

> BIN [*been*] places the action in the distant past (relative to the present axis) and/or that it expresses 'total completion of the event' . . . However, this gloss, and the semantic notion of a totally completed action in the distant past, is appropriate only for a subset of the data—those in which BIN is followed by non-stative verbs. With stative verbs, or with either kind in the progressive, the function of BIN is different. Instead of expressing completion of the associated process (a cover term for action or state) it asserts only that it began in the distant past and is still very much in force at the moment of speaking. (1975 : 170–171)

As we can see from all the *been* examples above, especially from the last two, each sentence complies with the preceding definition, thereby suggesting that *been* is unique to street speech.

There are some compelling facts that correspond to stressed *been* which help account for its unique status in black street speech. Rickford conducted an experiment where he collected subjective reactions to stressed and unstressed forms of *been*. Informants were asked to compare sentences like "She been married" versus the stressed form "She *been* married." Those who were familiar with black street speech referred to the first, unstressed sentence as a prior state of affairs, while the stressed form indicated that the marriage is well established and still active at the present time.

In other words, the stress on *been* is phonemic in black street speech and therefore capable of changing the meaning of the word. The single dimension of stress alone is sufficient to maintain this semantic distinction. By way of analogy, several of the African tone languages exhibit similar phonemic stress patterns, where modifications of tone constitute different semantic meanings. It would appear, at least in this case, that the slaves introduced this phonemic stress alternation, since other dialects of English have not employed stress as a phonemic (that is, semantic) boundary. Additional evidence will be needed before definitive conclusions can be reached on this point. The synchronic evidence, which was introduced by Rickford and reinforced by the adult uses observed here, suggests that stressed *been* is unique to street speech and Caribbean varieties of creole English.

Multiple Negation   Wolfram (1969) has observed that working-class adults in Detroit use multiple negation far less frequently than do teens and preadolescents in the same area. Our findings are quite similar with respect to adult street speakers across America, who modify their use of multiple negation in different situations. In some instances multiple negation has been observed in formal situations, and exceptions of standardized negation occur in other, less formal circumstances. However, the general trends for multiple negation find increased use in colloquial contexts.

As with other dialect differences marked by grammatical variation, it is relatively difficult to establish equivalent standard English sentences. With this limitation in mind, Labov (1972a) has developed a series of rules to identify restrictions on the kinds of negative formations that can be used in English dialects generally. We can now demonstrate that street speakers apply different rules for negation depending on the immediate speech event.

Before proceeding, let us consider what this increased awareness of negation implies with respect to communicative competence. Multiple negation is apparently one aspect of the vernacular that speakers can consciously manipulate, and they typically produce multiple negatives in circumstances where little or no stigma is associated with their use. At the same time, most of the consultants were capable of producing standardized negation in the full range of specified speech event types; that is, they had the capacity to apply alternating rules for negation at will.

Detailed discussions of the rules that govern negative constructions in both standard and nonstandard dialects of English have been presented by Labov and his colleagues (1968), Labov (1972a), Wolfram (1969), and Wolfram and Fasold (1974) and need not occupy additional space here. In order to expose the complex relationship between standard and nonstandard negation, Labov observed that the rules for negative attraction and negative agreement can be applied to generate acceptable sentences in either dialect. By way of illustration, I recorded the following sentences from a young woman who was angry at the prospect that another woman, a rival, would be going to an amusement park with a man whom both of the women liked. Before leaving with this man, the rival stopped at the pool to show off some new clothes that she had purchased for the occasion. Part of her attire consisted of a new pair of platform shoes, and when the couple finally departed the first woman uttered the following remark:

> It ain't no way no girl can't wear no platforms to no amusement park.

Certain rules are required to generate the multiple negatives that appear in this model sentence. Following Labov (1972a:133), we see that the *no* in "no girl" corresponds to an underlying indefinite *any*. Further, this *no* is linked with negative attraction that is derived from other negatives in the sentence. Placing this problem in its proper grammatical context requires a sense of how the rules of negative attraction operate for English generally. For the most part the linguistic rules which apply to standard English are directly applicable to the multiple negatives at hand.

The reader is, of course, directed to Labov's original analysis for more in-depth discussion of the value and limitations of the corresponding linguistic rules. From the standpoint of situational style shifting, in addition to rule restrictions that can be established vis-à-vis internal linguistic constraints, street speakers demonstrate that communicative competence goes beyond the traditional bounds of internal linguistic processes; this is seen in adaptations of linguistic behavior that are induced by the presence of particular participants in any given speech event.

To illustrate further, let us turn to some of the negative constructions that were produced in less formal speaking situations:

> Not none of my people come from up north.
> They didn't never do nothing to nobody.
> It ain't no brother of mine can't help us in hard times.
> I ain't never heard nothing bout no riot in Fernando.
> It ain't no brothers or Mexicans can't dance.
> You didn't win no city [championship] in '62.
> He ain't not never gon say it to his face.
> They can't do nothing if they don't never try.

While the preceding illustrations are only part of the large set of multiple negative sentences in the corpus, they are representative of the primary linguistic environments where multiple negation has been used. These examples are very similar in structure to the negative sentences that have been recorded by Labov and his colleagues in Harlem, as well as by Wolfram in Detroit. With this being the case, it is safe to say that the rules of negative concord and negative attraction are part of adult street speakers' competence, and these rules are retained by adult speakers who also learn rules for more standardized production as they grow older and expand their social networks.

Heretofore some scholars have assumed that contact with the standard dialect has influenced adult street speakers extensively, so much so that they are generally not expected to use vernacular styles. Dillard (1972:233–234) recorded a complementary observation from one of his twelve-year-old informants. The boy made distinctions between peer group language and the language used at home. Dillard attributes the confusion that the child faced to the foreign nature of the linguistic interview. I have made a similar observation pertaining to language changes in the peer group and the home: there is far more slang associated with peer language, and usually more cursing is attached to the peer group vernacular; home speech has much less slang and few—if any—curses. However, both styles are still representative of street speech and should not be confused with standard English (compare Folb 1980).

Returning to the examples of multiple negation, we are now prepared to modify the assumption that adult street speakers unilaterally drift toward the standard; rather, they develop a more refined communicative competence, one that allows them to employ different rules for negative constructions based on the likelihood that a particular sentence will be more or less stigmatized on any given occasion. By contrast, in more formal contexts, the same consultants produced sentences with standardized negation like the following:

> I'm not talking about any special person.
> We're not causing any trouble.
> You can't blame them for conditions they didn't create.
> She's not concerned if it doesn't affect her directly.
> They'll try to take anything that's not nailed down.
> . . . anybody that's not concerned about individual people has
>   no business in any kind of public office.

The preceding sentences are not an exhaustive list, but they are exemplary of the linguistic environments where most standardized sentences occurred.

Taken collectively, these observations suggest that adult street speakers have consciously recognized the situational stigma that can be attached to multiple negation, and their speech in different circumstances confirms this point. What is not so clear is the fact that stylistic options are not categorical across (in)formal speaking contexts. The important matter here is that the observed variation is heavily weighted in favor of more standardized rules in formal situations, with the option to use nonstandard negation in less formal situations.

Another dimension to the conscious control over multiple negation has to do with the amount of attention that it receives in school. Most of us are aware of double and multiple negatives and have good intuitions regarding grammatical sentences that use *ain't*; however, under the prescriptive guidance of well-intended educators, we also know that *ain't* and multiple negatives are unacceptable in writing or formal speech. It is therefore possible—and, perhaps, likely—that the overwhelming attention that negation has received outside of the black community, among teachers and logicians alike, has reinforced the stylistic sensitivity of adult street speakers.

Aspectual Marking with *Steady* Thus far we have examined grammatical constructions in street speech that are well documented in the existing literature. Now we come to *steady*, an aspectual marker having a unique status in street speech. Aspect influences the manner in which an activity or process is conducted. The following discussion is more directly related to identifying the grammatical status of *steady* than to examining any stylistic implications for its use. Here we will consider two main issues: what is the function of *steady*, and how did it come to be used in this way? The data are drawn from two primary sources, including natural usage during recorded interviews as well as responses to a questionnaire. While the orientation here is a synchronic one, a similar usage of *steady* has been observed in Caribbean varieties of English. These attestations lend support to the viability of the creolist origin hypothesis for black street speech, although the precise history of *steady* reflects several stages of development.

One of the primary reasons why *steady* has not appeared in the existing literature for street speech is presumably due to its shared characteristics with standard English *steadily*. *Steady* is also a camouflaged form, similar to modal *come* in street speech (compare Spears 1982). A camouflaged form is one that is shared by more than one dialect of a language; however, some dialects maintain unique grammatical and/or semantic qualities. There may be some overlap, with respect to shared functions for these forms, but they must maintain distinct characteristics that are not common to all speakers of the same language. In this case there are shared surface distributional similarities with standard English, but at the same time *steady* serves a unique aspectual function for black street speech.

Steady typically occurs with progressive (that is, verb+ing) verbs in sentences like "Leon steady trippin," "We be steady hustlin," or "She steady be runnin her mouth." The noteworthy exception has been observed with prepositions following *steady*, for example, "You just steady on everybody's case." Used in the preceding ways, *steady* functions as an intensified continuative. It can also be distinguished from other continuatives (for example, *always*) because the notions of consistency and persistence are not inherent or explicit with other continuative verbs. Compare "He always messin with somebody" and "He steady messin with somebody." In the first instance the sentence refers to all occasions, while the second focuses on how the action is completed on a single occasion. Additional examples of *steady* were recorded in natural conversation:

> Ricky Bell be *steady* steppin in them number nines.
> . . . and we be *steady* jammin all the Crips.
> . . . you got a mind inside of you that's . . your mind is *steady* workin.
> Them fools be *steady* hustlin everybody they see.
> He all the time be *steady* bitchin bout somethin.
> She *steady* be runnin her mouth [preposed *steady*].
> Them brothers be rappin *steady* [clause-final *steady* with heavy stress].

As demonstrated in the last two sentences, this general structure has some flexibility, but the most common syntax is best illustrated by the first five sentences. To focus on the general structure, then, where *steady* typically occurs the subject—a noun phrase—is always animate; every recorded example also referred to human subjects. The only restriction on the preceding noun phrases is that those with indefinite articles are ungrammatical; thus, "*A boy be steady rappin" is altogether unacceptable. *Be* in this environment is the distributive *be* that has been discussed previously in this chapter and elsewhere. The semantic nature of *be* in this context is directly associated with the progressive verb in the sentence. *Be* does not automatically carry a durative and/or habitual meaning; rather, depending on the verbal sentence, the relative habitual or durative function relies very much on the semantic intention of the corresponding verb. A sentence like "She be steady dancin" can carry either a durative or a habitual interpretation, depending on the context. It is therefore useful to think of *be* as reinforcing the habitual or durative orientation of the corresponding verb, and, as we can see from the preceding example, these distinctions come uncomfortably close together at times.

Steady is a predicate adverb which has the unique aspectual function of indicating that the action of a particular verb is conducted in an intense, consistent, and continuous manner. The function of *steady* is unique among the continuative aspect markers available in street speech, because there are no other continuatives that automatically carry these three semantic functions.

When twenty-seven white speakers were provided with questionnaires on *steady*, in nearly every case their intuitions equated the semantic functions with actions that are carried out *steadily*. While this is a close semantic approximation, the corresponding impact of intensity and continuation is not explicit when paraphrasing with *steadily* in the environments where *steady* is usually found.

The aspectual function of *steady* is predominant with progressive verbs. In Prince's analysis (1975) of aspect these are called "being" verbs, and they have the special characteristic of association with actions that are perceived as a process. Sag (1973) has similarly revealed important distinctions between the grammatical acceptability of stative as opposed to progressive verbs. *Steady* almost always occurs with progressive verbs that can be part of a process. More directly related to our findings with *steady*, most speakers readily accept such sentences as these:

We be *steady* running.
They be *steady* jumping.
He be *steady* sleeping.

On the other hand, most speakers reject clear stative cases:

*They be *steady* knowing the truth.
*He be *steady* resembling his mother.

There appear to be some interrelated historical implications associated with this usage. In this instance I believe that *steady* represents a reinterpreted form which must be distinguished from straightforward word substitution processes, that is, where we find a one-to-one correspondence between lexical items in the native and second languages. This particular reinterpretation process would have gradually emerged as slaves began to adopt *steady* as an aspectual marker. But this still does not address the larger question of how or why this particular interpretation was chosen.

It is important to again emphasize that black slaves learned English under circumstances very different from those of any other migratory group to the United States. The most extensive contact was either with slave overseers, who usually spoke nonstandard Scots-Irish dialects, or with other slaves, who, of course, spoke highly nonstandard English as well. Once again, slaves were not allowed to preserve their native language in transitional bilingual communities. Beyond these demographic considerations lies the fact that several of the Bantu languages employ aspectual markers that perform very similar functions to that of *steady* in street speech.[2]

These findings suggest that we have an overlapping of two dialect systems. On the one hand, we see that *steady* is unique to street speech, having historical traces in African languages like Bantu. In addition, similar constructions appear in other New World creoles like Guyanese creole and Bahamian English (John Rickford and John Holm, personal communication). In diachronic terms we can identify aspectual functions that are in part attributable to the African origins of street speech. Yet we also see innovative functions occurring with English verbs that preserve the general English paradigm for progressive versus stative verbs.

Steady, almost more than any other aspect of street speech, demonstrates that linguistic influences on the contemporary black vernacular can be deeply rooted in both African and Anglican sources. In light of the fact that *steady* appears infrequently in the corpus, it would be counterproductive to speculate about the implications of the presence or absence of this feature with regard to linguistic style shifting. *Steady* has been recorded only in familiar speech events (that is, types 1 and 3) where speakers were well known to one another, but this observation should not imply that we might not expect to find *steady* in more formal speaking contexts among the newly acquainted. Above all, *steady* reveals an important distinction between aspect in street speech and standard English.

2. In Zulu, for example, Welmers (1973: 331) identified a bound morpheme that indicated continuation of an action—that is, /-gide/. Another significant dimension of this morpheme is that it conveys progressive action—compare /ru/ = "work" and /rugide/ = "keep on working." Similar morphemes can be found in Swahili and other members of the Bantu language family. Additional support for this African-related influence can be found in several creoles. Voorhoeve (1962: 45–47) has described continuative aspectual prefixes in Sranan that qualify the nature of the verb's action. And speakers of Trinidad creole actually use /stʌdi/ in ways that are similar to *steady* in street speech (Ian Hancock, personal communication). Taylor (1977: 51) also identifies aspectual markers in Island-Carib that distinguish habitual, iterative, and durative aspect.

These observations are nevertheless preliminary and suffer from the limitations that scant, or unreliable, documentation possesses for sound historical reconstruction. However, in spite of these admitted limitations, the synchronic vibrancy of *steady* is prevalent and substantial. The majority of adult street speakers were familiar with *steady*, although not all consultants were clear as to who used it (as an aspectual marker) and who did not.

Grammatical Summary

Six syntactic aspects of street speech have been identified, based on natural occurrences within the conversational corpus: invariant *be*, perfective *done*, future perfective *be done*, stressed *been*, multiple negation, and aspectual marking with *steady*. With the exception of *steady*, which is introduced here for the first time, these grammatical issues are well documented in the existing literature on black English.

In many respects the findings discussed here do not represent new syntactic discoveries. The significance of these observations lies more in the realm of appreciating the fact that adult speakers retain and use vernacular grammar in colloquial settings. This might seem to be obvious and therefore of little interest; however, there has been considerable confusion about the role of adults with regard to vernacular usage and the evolution of street speech. By demonstrating that adults have developed a level of communicative competence that allows them to define the situation and then adopt linguistic behavior appropriate to that situation, we can establish a much clearer picture of how black street speech functions across age groups in other black communities.

When I first became interested in this problem, I had the opportunity to attend a lecture given by J. L. Dillard at Haverford College. At that time I asked him whether his analyses of black English, which were largely based on children's speech, were truly representative of the overall vernacular. His response, echoed in his book *Black English*, was that adults were poor informants for vernacular analyses because they had typically been too strongly influenced by exposure to standard English (see chapter 3).

The value of these long-term findings gives us a different perspective. Adult street speakers are not making unilateral adjustments in the direction of standard English; more correctly, they gain a refined communicative competence, with the ability to use standardized speech selectively. In turn, because the home environment represents the most colloquial of vernacular settings, there is a strong possibility that black children's language is influenced by colloquial adult speech, which is eventually reinforced in the peer group setting. Dillard's position that children represent the best informants merely reflects that fact that they have not yet developed the linguistic maturity to alter their vernacular styles in the presence of outsiders.

7
Phonological Variation

This chapter examines phonological variation. The title may be somewhat misleading, however, because most of the examples have grammatical status of one form or another. There are two main reasons why I have chosen to examine the linguistic variables in this chapter. First, they occur frequently in speech; as such they can be examined quantitatively with a high degree of statistical reliability. Second, this type of frequency can in turn be measured based on our speech event categories, thereby revealing any subtle changes in situationally influenced speech styles. Such evidence can also be used in future studies that compare various English dialects.

A well-known example of a linguistic variable is that of postvocalic /r/, which was studied by Labov (1966) in great detail among New Yorkers of different social backgrounds. Most Americans recognize the stereotyped pronunciations of New Yorkers who say *ca* for *car* and *pak* for *park*; the list could of course go on. Postvocalic /r/ is a linguistic variable because speakers do not always pronounce it, even for alternate renditions of the same word. Phonological variables can therefore be thought of as fluctuating pronunciations of particular sounds in language (for example, phonemes and morphophonemes). The task at hand for black street speech is to locate suitable variables and measure the frequency with which different pronunciations are used in relation to the speech event types. Here we concentrate most on phonology, although syntactic variation and lexical variation exhibit similar fluctuations in some instances.

Thus far we have seen that social circumstances can play a significant role in grammatical variation and specialized lexical marking. We now turn to smaller units of language. Most of the examples that we will be discussing here are well documented in the available literature, although no one has examined these variables with respect to their situational sensitivity. Several technical decisions had to be made with respect to the transcription of the data, the development of a suitable computer code to analyze the data, and the theoretical orientation of the corresponding software that I used for this study. Most of these details are tedious in nature and would serve the needs of only a few fastidious readers. I have discussed these issues at length elsewhere, and interested readers should refer to those works (Baugh 1979, 1980).

In the remainder of this chapter I will present the essence of the phonological findings, in the hope that readers will arrive at a clear sense of the nature of style shifting among adult street speakers. It is worth noting, nevertheless, that nonstandard dialects—by virtue of their isolation from more archaic (prescriptive) forms of standard speech—offer useful data for an examination of linguistic change and prevailing linguistic theories. The main reason why such evidence has not been fully utilized is rather simple: the very social isolation that is required to maintain linguistic (dialect) differences, to say nothing of the corresponding linguistic attitudes and stereotypes, is the very kind of isolation that causes street speakers to play hide-and-seek with their vernacular styles.

The decision to examine the same consultants repeatedly through the years was designed specifically to create a sense of familiarity, so that speakers could eventually feel (more?) relaxed while they were being recorded. As might be expected, some of the linguistic (that is, phonological) variables were sensitive to situational adjustment, while others were governed only by internal linguistic processes.

We will review several linguistic variables, including examples of suffix /-s/ variation, the contraction and absence of *is* and *are*, consonant reduction and loss at the ends of words (that is, /-t/ and /-d/), as well as the nature of postvocalic /r/ variation among street speakers. As mentioned, these examples are not merely phonemes of English, consisting of inconsequential sounds; the majority consist of cases where the linguistic variable also performs some grammatical function. The grammatical status of certain variables can be functionally vacuous in some sentences. For example, when a black child says, "I want ten cent," *ten* conveys plurality, and the omission of /-s/ to mark the plural eliminates functional redundancy. Plural /-s/ is therefore a linguistic variable for black street speech, because speakers occasionally use it or omit it.

It is important to emphasize the distinction between purely phonological variables, such as postvocalic /r/, where the variable does not have any grammatical status, and variation with a form like plural /-s/, where the phonology (the /s/ sound) intersects with the grammatical functions of conveying plurality. In other words, plural /-s/ is also a morpheme of English; it conveys semantic content when used in this way. This does not suggest that every /s/ in English has morphological (that is, semantic) content. Here we will consider cases where the grammatical function is well established in standard English but reflects greater variation among street speakers.

Suffix /-s/ consists of three distinct functions, each occurring at the ends of words: plural /-s/, possessive /-s/, and third-person singular /-s/. Each is represented by the following sentences respectively: "He has three books," "That's my brother's book," and "He likes books." Street speech tends to omit these functions of /-s/ quite frequently. These examples also demonstrate instances where suffix /-s/ has performed a redundant task. The information that /-s/ conveys is therefore vulnerable to omission, because it adds nothing to the content of the sentence, from a logical point of view. There are social consequences associated with capricious omissions of suffix /-s/ in speech or writing, but, again, from a purely logical standpoint we would expect redundant functions to be linguistically expendable. This is especially the case with phonological examples, like postvocalic /r/, where the variable has no grammatical status.

Because these linguistic variables are also phonemes, phonological units which are capable of changing the meanings of various English words, they would be expected to occur with considerable regularity. And, because they represent a small unit within any given word, questions remain regarding speakers' abilities to monitor their fluctuating usage of various phonemes. Thus, while we might accept the fact that street speakers control their vernacular grammar or colloquial pronunciations of particular (complete) words, it might be another matter altogether for them to overtly manipulate pronunciations of specific phonemes within words. The task might be made all the more difficult if the linguistic variables are difficult to hear and/or perform redundant grammatical functions.

The objective of the phonological study is to establish the pattern—or lack thereof—of linguistic variation, based on a quantitative study of the variables that have been mentioned, with respect to the four speech event types. This kind of phonological variation, which accounts for some of the major differences between street speech and standard English, is a delicate linguistic process.

The final results demonstrate that, in some instances, like those affecting suffix /-s/, strong social forces influence the form. Other examples, like the loss of final /-t/ and /-d/ as past-tense markers— for example, *-ed*, as in "He walked /wɔkt/ home" or "They climbed /klaymd/ over the fence"—are not sensitive to social influences. Past-tense /-t/ and /-d/ are affected most by the immediate linguistic

environment. The essential observation is consequently very interesting, because some of these variables are responding to social
forces, while others are not. This kind of information gives us a better sense of the nature of street speech styles, as well as a sense of
what speakers control versus what is controlled by internal linguistic properties.

Suffix /-s/ Variation

As indicated, suffix /-s/ serves three functions in English, including
plural /-s/, possessive /-s/, and third-person singular /-s/. In spite of
these diverse functions, street speakers vary their use of suffix /-s/
depending on the speech event. This has been a theme throughout
the book, but, with the long-term data in hand, we have the advantage of large samples of these linguistic variables and can subsequently determine patterns of behavior with greater accuracy. In
general terms suffix /-s/ is more likely to be absent during vernacular conversation and will be used with greatest frequency in more
formal speech. Internal linguistic constraints play a relatively minor
role in whether or not suffix /-s/ is used, especially when compared
with the verb *to be* or the absence of /-t/ and /-d/.

The analytic procedure is quite similar for all the phonological
analyses. We will outline suffix /-s/ in greater detail to clarify the
general method. An explanation of probabilities is therefore in order.
Probabilities determine the likelihood that an event will occur, just
as we can determine that a fair coin toss has an equal probability of
heads or tails. The computer programs that have been developed for
data of this kind identify the relative probability that specified linguistic and/or social factors affect the presence or absence of a particular linguistic variable. The selection of these categories of factors is critical; detailed discussion of the pertinent theoretical issues
can be found in an earlier publication (Baugh 1979 : 118). Two major
categories have been analyzed with respect to their probabilistic impact: the immediate linguistic environment, such as surrounding
phonological context and linguistic form, and the speech event in
which the data were produced. Because language is a by-product of
social evolution, it is subject to constant change and growth. It is
largely for this reason that probabilities are useful; the analytic
model does not make predictions beyond the observed data, yet it
has special subroutines to determine the statistical reliability of the
findings.

The linguistic constraints for suffix /-s/ are divided into two factor groups: consonants and vowels that immediately follow /-s/ as

well as phonological factors that immediately precede /-s/. The preceding phonological factors consist of nasal— (*cans*), voiced consonant— (*reads*), voiceless consonant— (*picks*), final /-ts/ cluster— (*lists*), and vowel— (*knows*). Each of the situational factors has, of course, been classified by speech event type. The criteria for the speech events were chosen, at least in part, because they can be equally verified for the entire data base. While other social and/or personal criteria inevitably play some role in linguistic behavior, they are beyond the scope of precise measurement and have been omitted here. A general pattern for situationally influenced styles has been revealed, nevertheless, as illustrated in figure 7. It may be useful to repeat the definitions of the speech event types. Type 1 consists of speech between familiars who share membership in the vernacular black culture. Type 2 occurs with less well acquainted individuals who share membership in the vernacular black culture. Types 3 and 4 take place with outsiders to black street speech. Type 3 includes familiar outsiders, such as shopkeepers or schoolteachers, while type 4 is the most distant and formal (see chapter 3).

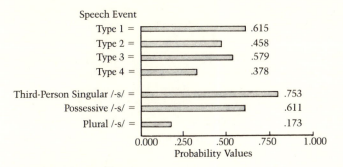

7. **Suffix /-s/ absence**

In order to understand the graphs, some additional background is necessary. The probability analyses examine each selected category as if it were statistically independent, although this does not imply independence in the real world. The final product is a series of numerical values that indicate the relative influence of any specified constraint on the linguistic variable under study. These probabilities, which are illustrated here for each speech event type, are weighted on a linear scale between 0.000 and 1.000. A value of .500 is neutral, 1.000 strongly favors omission, while 0.000 heavily preserves the linguistic variable. The values of greatest interest, then, are those farthest from the neutral .500 value, because they expose

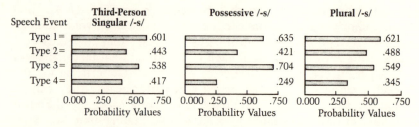

8. Speech event comparison for suffix /-s/ functions

the peaks and valleys of omission or retention. The same holds true
for all other variables in this chapter.

Suffix /-s/ is of considerable interest due to the strength of social
influence. The situational factors, that is, the speech events, are significant. The speech event values illustrated in figure 7 represent the
collective suffix /-s/ data. The other values in the figure correspond
to the probability that any given suffix /-s/ is likely to be one of the
three identified grammatical functions. Wolfram (1969) observes
that additional evaluations must be completed for the separate
grammatical functions, in order to determine the relative probabilities for each /-s/. Third-person singular /-s/ is the most likely to
be absent in street speech, while possessive /-s/ and plural /-s/ are
respectively favored to appear. The probabilities associated with
these three grammatical functions, illustrated in figure 7, are consistent with the pattern that Wolfram describes for Detroit. Once again
we find evidence for linguistic cohesion of street speech across regions and age groups. While the same linguistic environments are
favored, the adult consultants gravitated toward street speech
among familiars. This was initially a surprise to me, because I had
expected the speech styles to divide along the speech community
axis, which corresponds closely to racial lines as well; this preliminary assumption was wrong. This fact is driven home when the separate /-s/ functions are analyzed, as presented in figure 8.[1]

In spite of the fact that possessive /-s/ occurs proportionally
more frequently than third-person singular /-s/ and less frequently
than plural /-s/, the relative influence of the speech event types is

1. For the sake of clarity, figure 8 focuses on the relative influence of
the speech event types to the exclusion of other, less significant linguistic
factors. A more thorough exposition of the complete results can be found in
Baugh 1979.

preserved. In every case familiarity registers a clear preference for street speech, while formal styles are more common among the less well acquainted. The regularity of this social impact is remarkably uniform. More important, however, it strongly indicates that speech community membership is less likely to trigger colloquial speech styles than is the familiarity of the speakers. This is an important point, and we will return to it later when we consider the social and educational issues that surround contemporary black street speech.

Consonant Cluster Reduction

Having just looked at a case affected by social factors, we now turn to an example where they show no significant impact. Often, /-t/ and /-d/ are reduced as part of final consonant clusters in English. Occasionally these sounds are allomorphs that mark past tense—for example, *talked* /tɔkt/ or *filled* /fɪld/. The process of /-t/ and /-d/ absence in English is common to several dialects, but street speech once again displays some noticeable distinctions. Studies by Labov and his colleagues (1968), Wolfram (1969), and more recently Guy (1975, 1980) have looked at usage for black and white dialects. Following Guy's analyses, which are the most detailed, I have adopted his categorization of linguistic factors for this study.[2] Our situational factors remain the same throughout the investigation.

Like suffix /-s/, /-t/ and /-d/ are phonemes that—in certain linguistic environments—occasionally fill a grammatical role. These linguistic variables are nevertheless quite different as far as their rel-

2. The absence of /-t/ and /-d/ is another source of variation that is affected by a combination of phonological and grammatical constraints. Guy (1977) has written the linguistic rule for phonological variation of /-t/ and /-d/ as follows ($\emptyset$ = monomorphemic, + = ambiguous clusters, # = past tense):

(a) $/t, d/ \rightarrow \langle\emptyset\rangle/C\_\ \#\#$

(b) $/t, d/ \rightarrow \langle\emptyset\rangle/C \left\langle \begin{matrix} \emptyset \\ + \\ \# \end{matrix} \right\rangle \_\ \#\# \left\langle \begin{matrix} [+\text{consonant}] \\ [-\text{vocalic}] \end{matrix} \right\rangle$

The phonological factors that follow /-t/ and /-d/ register a broad range of influence. —Consonants, —liquids, and —glides are the most favored environments for absence. The preceding phonological elements that bolster this absence are sibilants— and stops—. The only surprise, if we can call it that, is found with the relatively low value associated with a following —pause; other vernacular studies show a much higher value. The most logical explanation at this stage is that speakers acquire different (that is, more standardized) linguistic norms as they grow older. Again, see Baugh 1979 for a complete presentation of the entire linguistic analysis.

ative sensitivity to speech event types is concerned. There are three pertinent grammatical categories to consider. The first consists of consonant clusters where final /-t/ and /-d/ do not have any grammatical status, such as with *past* and *cold*. The second case includes instances of "ambiguous" consonant clusters, where /-t/ and /-d/ are marking the past tense, but so too are changes in the pronunciation of the corresponding vowel. *Keep* versus *kept*, *tell* versus *told*, and *leave* versus *left* are good examples of ambiguous consonant clusters; both the vowel sounds and the final consonants change to indicate past tense. The final case is the one that has been discussed earlier in the chapter, namely, regular past-tense marking with *-ed*, as in *looked* /lʊkt/.

The situational and grammatical factors are displayed in figure 9. The probabilities associated with the speech event types hover close to the neutral .500 mark and are therefore insignificant. By contrast, when /-t/ and /-d/ indicate past tense, the probability that they will be uttered increases substantially. A glance at figure 9 reveals an important difference between this example and the cases of suffix /-s/ that were previously examined. In this instance there is a direct correspondence between grammatical function and the probability that the linguistic variable will be preserved in street speech.

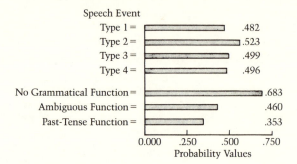

9. Final /-t/ and /-d/ absence

On the other hand, where /-t/ and /-d/ do not mark past tense, they are most likely to be omitted. Speakers are maintaining the functional distinction of tense marking, while eliminating final /-t/ and /-d/ when they do not serve a grammatical role or, to a lesser degree, when their function is ambiguous.

The main distinction that should be drawn between suffix /-s/ and /-t/ and /-d/ is that street speakers have pruned standard English, while taking care to preserve all its essential content. In instances where grammatical functions are important to conversational content, as with unmistakable past-tense forms, street speakers tend to preserve the linguistic variable with considerable regularity.

Is and *Are* Variation

Two of the most obvious sources of variation between street speech and standard English focus on the verb *to be* in the present tense, namely, *is* and *are*. Wolfram (1974) observed that *is* and *are* vary differently in street speech, and I have therefore analyzed the two separately. Elsewhere I have discussed this variation in more technical detail (Baugh 1980); a more complete picture of the historic and analytic implications can be found there. Some additional background is nevertheless necessary.

Although the majority of minority dialects, throughout the world, have been neglected in serious linguistic inquiry, the study of street speech has witnessed some of the most important theoretical developments in sociolinguistic studies. Labov's introduction (1969) of variable rules to linguistic science was based on a similar study of the black English copula (that is, the linking verbs *is* and *are*). During the 1960s, when the civil rights movement fostered a considerable amount of research in the general field of black American studies, educators and linguists concentrated their efforts on teaching black students how to learn and use standard English. Educational issues intersect with the study of *is* and *are* mainly because these variables received substantial analytic attention.

The related historical implications associated with these variables were touched upon in chapter 2, where the creolists and dialectologists presented alternative historical accounts of the same data. In early statements of the creolist position, Bailey (1965) and Stewart (1969) proposed that street speech did not have *is* and *are* as part of its underlying grammar. Contracted forms and, eventually, the complete words themselves would be introduced to older speakers who came into contact with standard English. The dialectologist position argues for the opposite historical case, assuming that street speech has the underlying *to be* verbs as an established part of its grammar. These established forms would then be subject to the same phonological and grammatical influences that affect comparable contractions of *is* and *are* in other colloquial English dialects. Labov's study (1972a) shows that street speakers can omit *is* and *are* in the same environments where standard English allows for the contraction of these forms.

The literature surrounding these linking verbs in black street

speech is substantial and, again, includes some of the most important analytic advances in sociolinguistic theory. From a more practical standpoint, both linguists and educators felt that they would
be better equipped to solve the mystery of the missing—or contracted—linking verbs if they could determine the evolution of the
forms. This information would in turn be used to develop effective
educational policies for black students.

Educational issues will be considered in greater detail in the
next chapter. For the moment we are more concerned with the analytic refinements that our long-term study with adults can reveal.
As mentioned, Labov (1969) and Wolfram (1974) have studied this
type of linguistic variation in the past, and their research concentrated exclusively on internal linguistic influences. This investigation introduces the speech event types as a new factor group, in an
effort to test the situational responsiveness of *is* and *are*. In this instance the social influences are somewhat haphazard and are less
significant to the distribution of variables than are the corresponding linguistic factors. The progressive revisions of the linguistic and
social factors for similar studies are presented in figure 10.

	Labov/Wolfram	Baugh 1980	The Present Analysis
Phonological Factor Group	-Consonant— -Vowel— —Consonant- —Vowel-	-Consonant— -Vowel— —Consonant- —Vowel-	-Consonant— -Vowel— —Consonant- —Vowel-
Grammatical Factor Group	Noun Phrase— Pronoun— —Gon(na) —Verb+ing —Predicate 　Adjective/Locative —Noun Phrase	Noun Phrase— Pronoun— —Gon(na) —Verb+ing —Predicate 　Adjective —Locative —Noun Phrase —Determiner # 　Noun Phrase —Miscellaneous	Noun Phrase— Pronoun— —Gon(na) —Verb+ing —Predicate 　Adjective —Locative —Noun Phrase —Determiner # 　Noun Phrase —Miscellaneous
Question Factor Group		Question Nonquestion	
Situational Factor Group			1. Familiar/Vernacular 2. Unfamiliar/Vernacular 3. Familiar/Nonvernacular 4. Unfamiliar/Nonvernacular

10. Factor revisions for street speech linking verb research

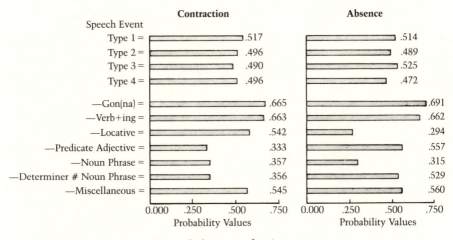

11. Variation—contraction and absence—for *is*

Figure 11, illustrating the situational and the grammatical probabilities for the contraction and absence of *is*, reveals that the speech
event types have little impact on overall usage. This pattern may
seem odd at first blush, but some related historical issues could account for it. Holm (1975) studied the grammatical hierarchy for linguistic factors that immediately follow the verb *to be*, that is, the
environments where we would expect to find *is*. Looking at Jamaican and Gullah English dialects, he found similarities in the environments that favored omission of the linking verbs. The pattern
is also preserved in the speech of Harlem teens, as illustrated from
my previous research on this form—see figure 12. Adult street
speakers, while using *is* with greater frequency than adolescents,
still favor reducing or omitting *is* in the same linguistic environments as do younger speakers.

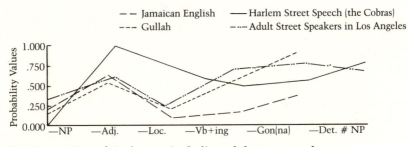

12. Comparison of *is* absence including adult street speakers

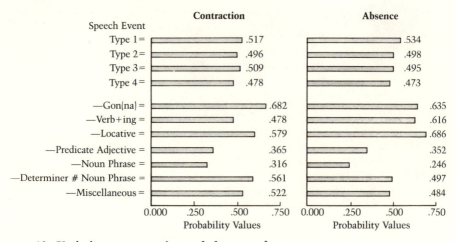

13. Variation—contraction and absence—for *are*

Are gives us a similar picture, but the situational factors seem to play a greater role—see figure 13. This is still somewhat puzzling; we will need additional evidence before an acceptable answer is found. As the evidence now stands, it appears that *are* variation is affected more by the immediate circumstances while *is* is constrained more by internal linguistic factors. The noteworthy difference for *are* variation can be found with two of the following grammatical factors: —locative and —adjective verbs do not correspond to the same probability relationships as do their counterparts with *is* (compare Baugh 1980:93). The —verb+ing and —determiner # noun phrase categories for contractions also differ greatly.

There is a logical explanation for the variable differences between *is* and *are*, although a complete thesis would occupy far too much space here. When *is* and *are* variation is compared, the similarities are more striking than the differences, but the differences lie in critical locations. The affected —locative and —adjective verbs occur in the very linguistic environments where Holm discovered similarities to Jamaican and Gullah dialects, yet it is in these same environments that street speech, for *are*, reflects similarities to white southern dialects. Fasold (1972) outlines a series of changes that demonstrate how the verb *to be* evolved in street speech. He hypothesizes that a substitution, where the word *de* changed to *is* in black street speech, took place first. Once this process was complete, *is* became subjected to the same phonological processes for contraction and omission that face other colloquial English dialects. Since the linguistic environments for *is* are not identical to those for *are*, the acquisition of these verbs was probably not completed during the same developmental period. Yet, because of the similarity in grammatical function and the common semantic trait of conveying no information, both *is* and *are* have continued to represent sharp points of contrast to standard English, especially formal varieties of standard English.

This same historical picture might account for at least a portion of the situational preference for *are* as well. If *are* became part of the street speech lexicon later than *is*, the circumstances surrounding the necessary exposure for linguistic incorporation probably changed as well. Exposure to schools, for example, where teachers were attempting to instruct students in standard English, would inevitably increase awareness of dialect differences that stood in obvious contrast to the standard. This kind of speculation, while not based on hard linguistic facts, is an effort to piece together the available fragments into a feasible scenario. Another possibility might be that *are* developed an increased sensitivity to social contexts because street speakers associated it with formal speaking contexts, thereby reinforcing slight situational trends in street speech.

Postvocalic /r/ Variation

Postvocalic /r/ occurs with considerable frequency in the corpus. The findings in this instance are more reliable statistically. The only major methodological modification has been to insure that no particular word has been counted more than twice in the speech of any consultant. For example, since some conversations focused on cars, consultants would have occasions to repeat the word *car* several times in a short segment of speech. If the individual said *ca* on all of these occasions, the findings could have been distorted. With this restriction in mind, the relevant factors consist of the following phonological environments, including —pause and the identified speech event types. These factors have been chosen for the sake of consistency with previous studies. The computer analysis indicates another case of situationally influenced variation, where the linguistic environment is less significant than the particular setting of each conversation. The pattern is clear from figure 14.

As with suffix /-s/, type 1 speech events among intimates favor the omission of postvocalic /r/, while the formal speech events of type 4 show the greatest use of /r/. Types 2 and 3 are quite similar in

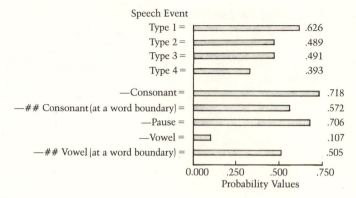

14. Postvocalic /r/ absence

this case. Consultants control their /r/ usage in ways that suggest overt manipulation. Street speakers are aware that /r/ omission is stigmatized outside of their immediate community, and their stylistic adjustments support this fact. Labov (1966) observed a similar trend in New York City. A complementary stratification of usage holds for black Americans as a race, but street speakers are likely to change their usage based more on the social context.

Summary of Phonological and Morphological Variation

Since suffix /-s/ and postvocalic /r/ indicate the strongest situational variation, while *is*, *are*, and /-t/ and /-d/ variation is much less situational, the logical question is why? The simplest answer is not simple at all, which is to be expected when the full range of influences is considered. The answer has been alluded to, although not stated explicitly. Postvocalic /r/ in this study has no morphological status, with the exception of contracted *are*—which has been analyzed separately. That is, there is very little meaning associated with the /r/ sound; thus *car* and *ca* will mean the same thing in the proper discourse context. The loss of this particular sound will therefore have very little effect on meaning. A similar situation holds true for many of the suffix /-s/ forms. When a conversation focuses on possession or pluralization, there are typically several other discourse indicators of these facts; the semantic burden generally does not fall on these suffix forms alone. It is largely for this reason that they too are subject to omission and situational variation in street speech. Both these sounds are single phonemes which carry little if any information in ordinary speech. They are nevertheless detectable in conversation and serve to identify an individual's speech community membership. Adult street speakers have mastered the ability to manipulate these sounds, so that they occur with greater frequency in formal speech.

Is and *are*, on the other hand, are not so neatly explained. It would seem that these complete words should be controlled with the greatest ease. Given the fact that the situational influence is very slight for both forms of the verb *to be*, some other explanation is possible. Perhaps, as complete lexical items, *is* and *are* were quick to come to the attention of educators and concerned parents, who brought these forms to the attention of young street speakers. Once exposed to two sets of linguistic norms, street speakers would then be required to determine when these linguistic variables should be used. This task is made all the more difficult because *is* and *are* lack semantic content, as with postvocalic /r/; these forms are readily expendable with no real loss of content. At this stage it appears that the grammatical contexts are most significant, with a lesser phonological preference for alternating consonant and vowel syllables (compare Labov 1972a). Such influences would account for the shared pattern of variation that we have observed among street speakers throughout the United States, as well as with Caribbean English.

Less mysterious is /-t/ and /-d/ variation, because there are unmistakable phonological or morphological roles associated with the appropriate linguistic environments. When /-t/ and /-d/ serve to mark the past tense, as in *left* and *talked*, there is a greater chance that the sound will be used—regardless of the speaking context. Once /-t/ and /-d/ have no semantic value, as with *lost* and *bold*, they are more likely to disappear, resulting in pronunciations like *los* and *bol* in street speech.

These phonological analyses, almost more than any other dimension of street speech, demonstrate the complexity and elasticity of the dialect. In many cases we find that street speech is in the forefront of certain linguistic changes for standard English, due to the elimination of redundant grammatical functions. On the other hand, with cases like the linking verbs, we find that speakers preserve traces of historical patterns that can be explained only through the gradual transmission of variable linguistic usage from one generation to the next. Thus, while some black children may now be exposed to street speech for the first time, having no insight into the language of their slave ancestors, those who grow up in areas surrounded by street speech (or rural black speech) are more likely to adopt the linking verb patterns of those who are around them. This process in turn serves as a telescopic link in the historical preservation of modern black street speech.

The linguistic alternations that are situationally influenced occur with linguistic variables that have minimum utility. While this trend is not categorical, it is significant and can serve as a foundation for linguistic changes in the future. When viewed collectively, lexical variation, unique grammatical constructions, and phonological variations comprise three major sources of linguistic difference between street speech and standard English.

The phonological patterns that we have observed are not tidy, but they reveal that different forces operate on street speech simultaneously. It would appear that speakers are capable of controlling their usage of some linguistic variables, while other variables are not monitored during ordinary conversation. The available evidence is insufficient to allow us to draw strong conclusions; in fact, it indicates a linguistic community that is in a state of rapid change. From a practical point of view we can see why such change might exist among black Americans, having been discriminated against on longstanding racial and linguistic grounds. And, as more blacks who speak standard English are represented through the mass media, the impression that standard English is essential to traditional American success will continue to be reinforced with increased regularity. The negative stereotypes associated with street speech have likewise been exploited through the mass media, although both impressions distort the true complexity of black American speech patterns.

In spite of these admitted limitations, my original objective remains the same. These particular linguistic variables have been selected for analysis because they can be measured with a high level of accuracy. Such precise measurement is rarely afforded to human behavior, which is one of the reasons why linguistic science has progressed as rapidly as it has. Future linguistic investigations will, of course, want to consider prosodic features, as well as pitch, stress, and intonation. At this stage of analytic development I have chosen to emphasize highly measurable phenomena, in an attempt to achieve a more objective impression of black street speech.

The remaining chapters will consider some of the social realities that confront street speakers as they compete for survival in American society. When I first began this study, I had hoped that linguistics could provide some solutions to the social problems that affected blacks and other linguistic minorities in the United States. I now realize that such a goal is too ambitious, at least based on the limitations of our linguistic knowledge. It is equally fallacious to assume that we must wait until we have a complete record of street speech—or other minority dialects—before we can offer useful suggestions to nonstandard speakers who want to participate more fully in American society. What follows in chapters 8 and 9 are preliminary attempts to examine the social pressures that are accentuated through the existence of black street speech and to offer some preliminary suggestions for those who are sincerely interested in greater social—and linguistic—accommodation among the general citizenry.

8
Educational Insights

As it is with so many others who have experienced the double blow of discrimination and poverty, the educational outlook for the majority of black children is still bleak. The usual practice is to focus attention on the schools: what are the teachers doing or not doing? The magnitude of this problem is far too great for another survey of the literature. My remarks are designed for concerned people, no matter what their race, who are dedicated to improving the future of our children. The intellectual resources that are available to blacks are greater than they have ever been throughout American history, but this fact can be misleading. Getting a good education will continue to be an uphill battle as school budgets shrink. For the language arts, in particular, the gradual public trend toward more minorities learning standard English on their own initiative may give the impression that no special help is needed. The style shifting that we have observed among adults, however, suggests that special linguistic problems should come as no surprise.

What follows is not directly associated with the linguistic evidence and style-shifting processes that we have reviewed. Adult street speech patterns have gradually emerged as a public (black) response to linguistic intolerance and other forms of racial discrimination. The majority of black parents whom I have interviewed through the years, spanning both poles of the political spectrum, overwhelmingly stress the past, present, and future role of education as a means of attaining a better life for themselves and their children. It is primarily due to the continued urgency of these educational needs that I offer these remarks and observations.

Street speakers, like all speakers, make on-the-spot adjustments in their speech. Due to the broader range of variation that exists between street speech and standard English, countless gifted minority students have been dismissed as poor intellectual risks. I don't mean to suggest that mastery of standard English assures success in school; thousands of white standard speakers have not fared all that well. Nevertheless, the competitive nature of our society rewards cultural homogeneity, and speaking ability is part of this process. In order to serve as many children as possible, the most immediate source of reliable help will continue to come from concerned people. An educational program or idea is only as good as the people who administer it; if their hearts are not in the enterprise, the self-fulfilling prophecies of failure will continue.

Educators face three general linguistic populations in our schools: children who learn standard English as their native dialect, students who speak nonstandard English, and others who are not native English speakers. In the past a variety of programs have been implemented to meet the needs of bilingual and bidialectal students. While all such programs are well intended, many are ill conceived and retard genuine progress. For example, it is my belief that trying to develop black readers in the vernacular is a bad idea. Before expounding my position I would like to share an anecdote that contains a pertinent analogy. A scholar from the People's Republic of China lectured to linguists and educators at the University of Pennsylvania. He talked about China's language policy, about how its government was active in trying to get all citizens to read and speak a common dialect. A Chinese-American graduate student expressed alarm at this prospect, pointing to the cultural and historical damage that would result from this linguistic homogenization. His reaction holds parallels for black Americans.

In the Chinese context, this scholar stressed fulfilling modern social needs while not losing sight of the richness of history: "In China we must feed 900 million people; we appreciate our history and linguistic diversity, but, like the beautiful robes of the ancient emperors, the language is a reflection of China's past. To feed our people today we must be able to change if we are to survive." I similarly appreciate the emotional ties that hold so many black people to their street speech roots. My emphasis is more narrowly concentrated on educational survival. It goes without saying that society is constantly undergoing change. The educational aspect of this change, however, is subject to a barrage of social, economic, and political factors. The linguistic picture is, by comparison, fairly straightforward. Street speakers are part of the nonstandard English population. The vernacular that black students bring into the classroom is unquestionably a dialect of English; the linguistic differences are nevertheless sufficient to cause social barriers even when effective communication takes place.

Education is vital to broader enculturation, for all groups in the society. Traditionally ethnic groups have helped "their own kind," and this is already a tradition in many black communities. Here I will be recommending ways to imitate aspects of a private school education. Limited enrollment and more teacher-student contact are two advantages that private schools can offer. At present a majority of black parents hope that their children will learn competitive (that is, marketable) skills in school, and many parents seek outside help for their children if they cannot provide it themselves. The problem, with respect to the broader vernacular population, is that this kind of assistance is unsystematic, and many talented people who would be willing to help simply have no place to turn. Mackler (1980) advocates community-based programs, and I echo his call. While it is vital to continue to demand the best education for children in the public schools, schools are subject to bureaucratic dictates. As such the wheels of change continue to move too capriciously and slowly to meet the immediate needs of today's students. In the short and the long term, more human contact will insure that fewer talented students escape recognition.

To return, then, to my concern about elementary texts written in the street vernacular, a close examination of such renditions reveals an important fact. It is helpful if the student already knows how to read standard English; otherwise many of the respellings and grammatical adjustments are confusing or unintelligible. For example, some contemporary writers have respelled *the* as *duh* for the black vernacular; presumably this new spelling is closer to the true pronunciation. The orthographic reality, though, has always tolerated discrepancies between pronunciation and spelling (for example, *knight* and *climb*). It therefore does black students very little good, as far as their own reading is concerned, to have words respelled at the expense of postponing exposure to the standard—to the dialect of traditional science, technology, and so on. While some linguists have called for vernacular readers, many black parents have rejected this practice and will continue to do so as long as they feel it hurts their children.

Practical help requires an appreciation of the present educational problems: the majority of black children attend overcrowded, understaffed, ill-equipped, and underfunded public schools. When the linguistic issues are added to this picture—where the standard dialect and the peer vernacular reinforce different linguistic styles—then the enormity of the task begins to crystallize. We can dismiss the antiquated notion that black children are inherently inferior. Outstanding teachers have shown how much can be achieved with a combination of hard work, motivation, and concerned parents.

Their combined efforts shatter the arguments of genetic inferiority, and these efforts are supported by a large and growing body of literature. The ultimate test of education lies in the competitive abilities of our children; we teach them to share their toys and to get along with others, but as adults only the strongest and most talented will obtain economic security and self-sufficiency.

The German sociolinguist Dittmar concludes his book with a chapter titled "Applied Sociolinguistics in the U.S.A.: The Variability Concept and Its Ghetto Specialist." He surveys the situation with the clarity that geographic distance and linguistic inquiry afford. The reader is directed to his work for a more complete discussion, but for the point at hand he outlines several pertinent truisms:

> In the U.S.A., the richest industrial nation in the world, there is a stark contrast between wealth and poverty; at the beginning of the 1960s two fifths of the American population—77 million people—lived in a state of chronic poverty.
>
> The hardest hit are the Blacks living in the ghettos, and other ethnic minorities such as Puerto Ricans, Chicanos, and Indians. There is a lack of jobs and the number of unemployed is increasing. The Blacks are the group most discriminated against in the labour market. . . .
>
> The avowed aim is to get the "social dynamite" under control and to adapt the Blacks (and other minorities) to the requirements of a highly-industrialized capitalist society engaged in international competition, i.e., to eliminate illiteracy and to satisfy the need for qualified workers (technicians, etc.). The measures taken are embellished with the principle of equality of opportunity, which should be guaranteed by a suitable educational system. The contradiction that exists between the demand for equality of opportunity and that for competitiveness is glossed over. Yet competition, "upward social mobility," is precisely the principle on which capitalist society is based. Little account is taken of economic and social inequalities which form each individual's starting handicap in the competitive society, and failure in competition is mostly attributed to *individual* shortcomings. It is typical that the motto should so often be "equality of opportunity," rather than "equality of results," although, under any rational assumption equality of results (achievements) averaged over various social groups would be the most reliable test for the success of the current social development programmes. One task of the educational system,

particularly that of compensatory education, is to conceal the fact that there exists a bias in favour of competition and against equality of opportunity. (1976:242–243)

In spite of the inequality of opportunity, blacks and other minorities have taken steps to become more competitive. Because the United States is the wealthiest industrial nation, the likelihood of eventual—albeit gradual—participation is greater than it has ever been. This participation still rests with the skills of individuals. As Dittmar observes, access to the best skills (for example, schools) is limited to an elite who can afford to purchase the (private) training. Since few minorities can buy this superior product, self-supporting strategies, which imitate private training, can aid minority groups as long as people are willing to commit their talents to such an enterprise. Some additional historical background serves to clarify the task.

Slaves were not brought to America to become scholars. Captive human labor at a competitive market price was the objective. Social control through purchase, race, and economic strength, rather than through inherent superior intellect, nurtured the social abyss between black and white America. Hall and Freedle (1975) examine several of the social, psychological, and cultural factors associated with a transitional black population—a population of freed captives in a racist society. Slavery also disrupted black families, and the love of parents for their children was historically used as a weapon for social control. Add to this historical climate the fact that it was illegal to teach slaves to read and write, and few should wonder why so many blacks are still less competitive than the majority population. Post–Civil War discrimination was severe throughout the United States and continues in some segments of society, in spite of the civil rights movement and the laws that have resulted from it.

It serves little purpose to go on about inequality. World history shows that inequity and injustice have been the rule more than the exception. The American dream, where hard work is rewarded, can still be achieved with the right combination of training, timing, and luck. Economic discrepancies will continue to plague most minorities, because access to the "best" schooling is not a right; rather, it will continue to be a privilege. In order to provide minority children with similar privileges, concerned adults will need to map out educational strategies, using a combination of human and fiscal resources in a prudent way. Teachers will continue to face a deteriorating situation in school districts where funds are reduced. Parents will need to take this into account as they develop supplementary programs for their children.

Those individuals who can afford to send their children to private schools will continue to do so, and my remarks may be of little use to them. Others, who want to help children attending public schools, will need to set up extracurricular programs. The nature of many classes calls for strict discipline; the best teachers find it difficult to educate under such conditions. Concerned parents who recognize these problems can coordinate extracurricular activities, which must be handled with extreme care. Too much of the wrong help can be worse than no help at all. While this may be hard to appreciate at first blush, minority students often receive mixed signals from parents, teachers, friends, and others.

We should consider a rhetorical question before reviewing what can be done to help minority children become more competitive: what would society be like if public education were successful, in the sense that minorities in fact became competitive with the existing social elite? I'm not sure of the exact answer, but society would surely be different from the one we now know. Most black consultants have discussed the dichotomy between gradual social change and the desire to have a piece of the action now. There is a theory of social relativity at work here. Those who suffer from economic hardship are, quite understandably, anxious about their own future and that of their children. In the context of economic recovery, fewer public revenues will be available for groups who do not have substantial financial holdings and/or political influence; this is just the way it is.

When I was growing up in Los Angeles, the first public school that I attended—Sixth Avenue School—was integrated with minorities: blacks, Chinese, Japanese, and a sprinkling of chicanos made up the population. Our immediate neighborhood was mixed primarily with blacks and orientals. Classes ended at 3:00 P.M., when most of us would walk home; others would stay to play on the school grounds. But the majority of the Japanese students did not have this luxury—they attended a private school for two hours after the public school closed. This self-help training for survival in America was a no-nonsense venture steeped with traditional cultural values. No government funding was given to this program, although many of the students were quite poor.

Slavery has splintered similar efforts among black Americans for several reasons. Parents are nevertheless united when the education of their children is concerned; they want the best combination of available facilities and resources. In order to achieve this end by, say, approximating a private school education, additional time and training will be required, in conjunction with the public school program. If students attend schools that do not assign homework, then parents or study groups will need to fill the gap. Some of the strategies that I am suggesting are not new; they have worked in isolated schools but have not received adequate attention (see Hoover 1978; Roueche 1981).

As an initial point of departure, parents, teachers, pastors, scout leaders, and so on should examine the texts that their children are using at school. In connection with this fact-finding effort, suitable educational expertise should be located. There are thousands of retired teachers who might be willing to help in this regard, and local colleges and universities may be willing to give students course credits for tutoring in extracurricular programs. Ultimately these educational consultants must work closely with parents at every stage, so that communication between all parties—including the students—remains high. This can provide one of the clear advantages that private institutions offer, namely, more individualized attention. The available materials should be examined closely. Public and school libraries can also be contacted to determine the availability of additional materials for students.

Publishers have recognized the desire of minorities to increase their training, and many have toll-free numbers which anyone can call to order free catalogs of different educational supplies. In group programs parents can pool their funds to purchase certain products collectively, sharing expenses and equipment among several families. All these suggestions require supervision and organization. In much the same manner that paramedics are not doctors, concerned adults may not be trained teachers. This lack of training is a limitation but should not prevent concerned people from providing needed help.

It would be naïve to assume that all minority children can receive voluntary support. As an initial point of departure, individual parents can work with their own children, while those who can organize educational co-ops can begin to form study groups that meet their children's needs. Students should be consulted periodically during this process, because they are keenly aware of what they are being exposed to at school. Each subject has received much attention from publishers, and books, tape recordings, photos, and so on should be readily available from several sources.

Various pilot studies have suggested that some type of immediate reward system for achievement, including modest prizes or certification, plays an important role in student motivation by heightening the sense of competition that is essential to success in adult society (see Bell 1980). To the extent that it is possible, extracurricular programs should incorporate modest rewards and recognition, because delayed gratification is often too abstract to serve as adequate motivation for young students. A series of structured contests can be used for this purpose (see Baugh 1981). The ultimate goal, however, is to develop improved educational skills for economically disadvantaged bidialectal or bilingual students.

Focusing on the language arts, motivational programs should try, whenever possible, to utilize existing recreational activities for pedagogical purposes. For example, young black girls are famous for their jump-rope rhymes. A series of contests could be developed to reinforce this poetry, thereby using a popular game to experiment with language. Other word games can be similarly designed to enhance basic language arts skills. I am not suggesting that we advocate play to the exclusion of serious schoolwork; rather, we should utilize the existing recreational activities whenever possible. Students are more easily encouraged to write lyrics and create songs when that is already part of their peer group activity.

Through a balanced program of traditional and innovative techniques, minority students can receive a better education than most have received in the past. The nature of future job markets will be such that race will be less of a barrier than it has been before now, although discrimination will inevitably persist in some circles. This change is due to the growing number of highly skilled minorities. As American business adjusts to meet the needs of future markets, both at home and abroad, a majority of jobs will require some technical training. Extracurricular programs will need to take this fact into account.

Technology strides forward, as do the changing job market and required training. The most fundamental of these technological changes involves the rapid advances that we have seen with computers, which are now common in many homes. In much the same way that the automobile transformed society, knowledge of computers and corresponding personal ownership will alter our lives in ways that we cannot yet fully grasp. The joint economic and educational reality still favors the status quo, because access to computers is another economic privilege. Extracurricular groups may want to put home computer purchases high on their list of necessary equipment, so that minority children are not left too far behind other children who have their own computers. Fortunately, vast numbers of companies continue to make computers cheaper and easier to use.

Technology aside, there is still no substitute for human assistance. The more time we sacrifice for our children's education, the better their chance for competitive survival. It is, of course, an unfair quirk of history that minority children must invest more time and energy to achieve educational parity, but this is as it has always been in the United States. There is a threshold to this assistance, though, because children are not robots. Too much help can destroy the very intellectual achievements that parents hope to reinforce. Parents should therefore listen closely to their children and take care not to saturate these extracurricular programs with too many tedious exercises. Extracurricular activities are at their best when students are eager to participate; also, as part of the process, children can improve their traditional educational performance.

With the language arts specifically, most programs where students engage in organized activities requiring some type of language skill will enhance overall linguistic proficiency. Spelling contests, songwriting contests, and contests involving deciphering the lyrics of popular songs can all be enjoyable while increasing the students' exposure to and facility with language. Again, many educational publishers appreciate this fact and have developed various products and programs to make learning more fun (see Simpkins and Holt 1977).

By rewarding tedious work with some kind of prize or recognition and by linking this to other activities that are fun for students, parents and program administrators will also become more involved in their children's education. This can only have positive benefits in the short and the long run, because a well-rounded education will not be left to chance or, worse, to the bureaucratic dictates of unpredictable resources. In situations where no money is available to purchase special books or equipment, parents can structure exercises and games for home use with the help of teachers, librarians, or trained (volunteer) consultants. The sacrifices that parents and students must continue to make are inescapable. In order to become competitive on a larger scale, blacks and other minorities must ultimately demonstrate that, by performing the same task or producing a better product, they are equal to or more skilled than anyone else who is qualified for the same job. Anything less will not succeed.

Behavioral science has a long way to go before definitive solutions to educational problems are developed. As indicated previously, today's student does not have the luxury to wait for tomorrow's solution. Those students who are fortunate enough to either make it on their own or receive supplementary assistance will have a better chance at success within the mainstream than those who do not. Through individual or group efforts, volunteers, parents, teach-

9
Impediments to Employability

The same kind of helping-hand approach that I advocate for education will also be needed to assist street speakers who strive to enter professions. My observations are based on evidence from two primary sources: prospective employers who expressed concerns about minority employees and black students or consultants who have sought information on how to learn standard English. As any student of political philosophy, race relations, or economics knows, these are very intricate issues, and linguistics is not a usual source of expertise in this area. However, during conversations and interviews with whites and blacks from the broadest backgrounds, some obvious trends emerged. Employers were seeking "articulate" blacks (and other minorities) to fill management trainee positions, or they were seeking quick-fix speech and writing courses for prospective clerical staff. In any case "articulate" speech in this instance translates into proficiency with standard English.

On the other side of the coin are those who came to seek help. They knew of the employers' needs (demands?) and were willing to make the necessary sacrifices to learn standard English. Based on the majority of interviews with blacks from all walks of life, it is clear that most acknowledge that "white speech" is necessary if one seeks to participate—as fully as possible—in the mainstream culture. I will be looking not at a lot of statistics or economic theories here but at the personal experiences of real people who expressed their ambitions and frustrations. This is not to suggest that I do not appreciate the impact of racism and poverty on black employability; rather, these topics have been debated at great length by others who are far more qualified to discuss them. Here we focus on the neglected population: street speakers who feel the economic pressures of limited options in a competitive society.

Most business managers are concerned with communication. "How can we get our people to communicate more effectively?" "Improved communication can only lead to improved productivity."

ers, and so on can attack ignorance from several fronts at the same time, while providing their children with a superior education.

Given these suggestions, logical questions remain regarding the relationship between linguistic style shifting and the education of children who speak street speech. Because street speech evolves in the home and peer settings, style shifting emerges as a dimension of normal language development for many urban black children. As such no formal instruction is needed, because these skills are learned in the social milieu. Labov (1982) has also found, using evidence from the Ann Arbor trial on black English, that most black parents want their children to learn norms for social assimilation and competitive, marketable skills. Undue emphasis on linguistic style shifting could easily be misleading and could distract students from the more pressing task of mastering the language arts skills that are essential for competition and greater social parity.

The language of American white-collar business, however, is standard English, and managers expressed the desire to hire people who have already developed effective proficiency. The concerns of managers were at their peak under government pressure for affirmative action; parenthetically, few managers expressed any difficulty communicating with middle-class white women. Minority women were considered to have the same language problems as minority men.

We must appreciate that strong social forces are at work here, because employers want—and need—to hire people they feel will be an asset; street speakers are usually dismissed as possible candidates for anything but unskilled or semiskilled labor. There are, of course, countless exceptions; this is nevertheless a prevailing view among nonblack managers who have had limited contact with blacks. In a sense these managers are a barometer reflecting the language attitudes of the larger society. The linguistic style shifting that we have witnessed has evolved, at least in part, due to the tacit recognition of a double linguistic standard for street speakers. Although most black consultants acknowledged this dialect dichotomy, it evoked a broad range of responses. Some felt a genuine frustration at their inability to shift easily in and out of standard English, while others claimed that they would never use "white speech" under any circumstances, and vice versa. As has been the case thus far, the true norm falls between these extremes.

I will be concentrating on the needs of street speakers who face the task of learning or improving their command of standard English. Since most of the people who desire to learn standard English are trying to enter professional fields, my comments will be focused on their needs. There are, of course, fascinating linguistic pressures affecting other workers, be they black or white, male or female, older or younger, but these are too pervasive for the discussion at hand. By concentrating on the professions, where blacks are still a rarity, I hope to provide information that can serve conscientious people, regardless of race. Managers will need to appreciate the tremendous linguistic task confronting street speakers, and street speakers must come to a fuller appreciation of what employers want in terms of linguistic proficiency.

Some of the clearest assessments of America come from foreign visitors. One scholar from Korea made the following observation regarding the vitality of American culture: "Here in America you are rewarded for becoming an American; if you talk, act, and adopt the customs you can be accepted. In my country the purity of your blood is critical; no matter how many customs you adopt, unless you are pure-blooded you will never be included." The linguistic differences that we have observed between street speech and standard English are the remnants of a slower enculturation rate for blacks. The racial boundary has been a special parameter for all nonwhites to some degree, whether by choice or by external exclusion. We have consequently reached an interesting point in the evolution of black speech patterns. Blacks are no longer excluded—in the sense of categorical exclusion—from the professional ranks. Many firms see themselves as being quite progressive because of a good affirmative action track record. Other firms couldn't care less. This is the reality that confronts all job seekers, and street speakers will be judged according to the employers' standards.

It may seem ironic, but many of the harshest critics of street speech are black. Scholars have typically pointed accusing fingers at upwardly mobile blacks, claiming that they were Uncle Toms or Aunt Jemimas who had turned their backs on those they left behind. My experience is somewhat different, although I would agree that some black critics have an "I made it, let them make it" attitude. But this simplifies the picture too much. There are pockets of criticism against street speech across the black social spectrum. If there is a common characteristic, it lies in the shared belief that speech, intelligence, and social background are tied together very closely. This should not be surprising, since it continues to be the prevailing view for the larger American society. In fact, some white managers have admitted privately that it is good policy to hire minorities in the personnel department. If minorities themselves maintain stringent standards for a firm, there may be less chance of overt discrimination problems. In any event, we have now arrived at a point in history where the management-worker boundary is no longer exclusively a white-black boundary.

The main caution that managers should observe involves keeping their criticism of street speech within reasonable bounds. Just as some people have more athletic ability than others, some are able to master dialects more readily than others. Since speech is a capricious indication of a person's full talents, it can—in many cases—be given a lower priority during preliminary probationary periods. This is not to suggest that we lower standards. Nothing could be further from my thoughts; rather, to tap the full human potential—especially in the growing technological age—greater linguistic tolerance can be an asset. Just because a person speaks street speech should not imply diminished intellectual potential. By the same token, street speakers must appreciate an employer's needs and strive to take the necessary steps to obtain the appropriate training.

Heretofore, dialect attitudes along with other social factors have stood as a genuine barrier to many minorities. For those managers who see this as a problem, it may be helpful to discuss this topic with applicants and employees, using ethnosensitive care. Because of the stigma that is and has been associated with street speech, this is an issue that can be very personal and could be highly emotional as well. What might seem to be a simple suggestion from a manager's viewpoint can translate into a complicated problem for an employee. The basic complaint that street consultants shared with respect to criticism of their speech, by teachers and employers, involved the patronizing manner with which the black dialect is usually treated: "They act like you dumb." It is my belief that we have not fully tapped the innovative potential of the broader citizenry. The creative spirit still thrives; the challenge entails overcoming the historical barriers that have restricted full participation by talented people in a truly competitive society.

When street speakers demonstrate the desire to participate, dialect barriers should not stand as the major obstacle to advancement. I recognize, of course, that proficiency in standard English is essential to some occupations. There are, nonetheless, many professions where standard English is not essential. In the final analysis, the demands of the job market will determine who lands a job and who does not. Managers must come to appreciate that a lot of hidden talent has remained hidden because of long-standing stereotypes.

Street speakers must also appreciate that, given a choice, most professional employers will continue to hire standard English speakers, especially in positions where public contact is involved. A casual glance at any major corporation will prove this point; those minorities who are in the public eye have typically mastered standard English to a great degree. Thus the psychological dimension of learning standard English can be a critical factor. In street culture, especially among males, masculinity is reinforced by the eloquence of one's rap. It goes without saying that street rappin' is foreign to most corporate boardrooms.

Aspiring black students and professionals can—in some instances—be steering a collision course between the vernacular dialect and employers' linguistic requirements. Furthermore, the older one is before making a sincere attempt to learn a second dialect, the more difficult the task becomes. I stress sincerity here, because any attempt to teach standard English will fail miserably if there is resistance on the part of students. Several emotional factors come into play here, one being the strong street stereotype that Uncle Toms and Aunt Jemimas are the primary speakers of black standard English. In spite of the fact that this is not true, the perception has had an impact on street speakers who want to maintain public allegiance to black culture. This loyalty, when combined with the stereotypes associated with black standard speakers, leaves many with the impression that if they learn standard English they will lose the ability to speak street speech. This just isn't so.

Some black university students once told me of an informal experiment: they spoke standard English during their visits home between semesters. The reactions from vernacular blacks were negative—the standard was perceived as "sadity" (that is, snobbish, lofty). Street speech was preferred in intimate settings. The style shifting that we have observed is part of the solution to this dilemma; individuals make gradual or abrupt changes in linguistic behavior to serve their immediate needs. Although I was interested in the result of this experiment, my field experience has taught me to avoid domestic confrontations whenever possible. Certainly, the notion of domestic conflict is another vital dimension of the problem. If, as I have suggested, proficiency with standard English cannot be achieved without practice, when will street speakers be able to practice, particularly if the vernacular is the dominant dialect in their lives? The best exposure—from a linguistic standpoint—is direct interaction with standard speakers. Such interaction can have the effect of dialect leveling and accommodation. If direct contact with standard speakers is not available, street speakers can work with tape recorders, using role playing or simulating standard utterances for the purpose of practice.

Just as musicians must train with their instruments for hours before playing in front of an audience, street speakers seeking greater proficiency in standard English will need to practice extensively before they are able to use it effectively in public. At this point the unilateral nature of the adjustment becomes clear. Pragmatic reality forces the burden of adjustment on groups who are outside positions of influence and power. It does little good to claim that street speech is a valid dialect—which it is—when the social cost of linguistic and other differences can be so high. Those blacks who were native street speakers, but who then learned standard English, can typically shift back to the vernacular with ease when the appropriate situation arises. The same holds true for many other ethnic or regional dialects in the United States. I have, of course, oversimplified the true linguistic picture for the sake of brevity. The linguistic style shifts are nevertheless a flexible component that is available to most black speakers to some degree. The second dialect is the one that usually poses the greatest difficulty: the native dialect can be preserved as long as there is periodic contact and a personal desire to hold on to it.

There are several preliminary exercises that street speakers, and perhaps managers, may find helpful as a point of departure for those who want to brush up on standard English. Here I will outline two such methods. To reemphasize a preceding point, the best exposure is direct and personal. When limited contact is available, however, certain verbal exercises can be helpful. The first requires no equipment; the second enlists tape recorders. A drill that is commonly used by drama and speech coaches consists of a rapid sequence of consonant and vowel combinations, as articulation exercises. The speaker chooses a consonant, say, /b/, and then places a /b/ sound in front of the long and short vowels. Taking the vowels in sequence, the student says *bay* /be/, *be* /bi/, *by* /bay/, *bow* /bo/, and *boo* /bu/. The sequence is then repeated with the short vowels. The vowels can also be placed before the consonant, and so on. Some sounds will combine to form words, while others will be nonsensical. Speech teachers suggest experimenting with these articulatory games, and they can be structured for various age groups.

Phonological exercises serve to free the student from the language; in other words, it is often difficult to hear how your dialect differs from someone else's unless you can step beyond the language. In this instance the nonsense syllables serve the purpose. While an individual can practice these exercises in private—while driving to work, for example—it is very helpful to have others provide periodic feedback on pronunciation and progress.

The second exercise, which also concentrates on verbal skills, requires the use of a tape recorder or, preferably, two tape recorders. Students should first obtain some recorded samples of standard English; broadcast speech could easily serve the purpose. Once a sample of speech is at hand, certain words and phrases can be chosen for repetitive practice. Most adult street speakers face a no-win situation to some extent, because complete mastery of standard English is hard—although not impossible—to achieve. I must reemphasize the need for students to be willing to participate if success is to be gained; unless there is a genuine desire to learn the second dialect, the motivation will be insufficient to withstand the tedious hours of practice.

The first phase of the second exercise requires the student to choose a selected word or phrase from the recording and to reproduce it as closely as possible. After sufficient practice, students should record their own speech and then critically compare the differences. Actors have used similar techniques when learning an accent for a particular role. I am not suggesting that blacks need to act in order to be competitive in the job market, but it is inevitable when a new role is demanded by employers. These exercises can help those who want to enhance their standard usage.

Attitudes and perceptions play such an important part in job-related matters that some discussion is essential. The exercises that I have outlined are largely cosmetic; they will not trigger any broad-based language arts improvement. Rather, because we are all judged in the immediate context of our productivity and performance, the ability to use the standard dialect can often be the difference between effective and ineffective communication. As we have observed repeatedly, these attitudes are a residue of racism, but the resulting pressure on blacks to "conform" has been tremendous throughout American history. Most readers already recognize the situations where both the standard dialect and the street vernacular are appropriate. The exercises are a good point of preliminary departure for students. Educators continue to make new discoveries for teaching language arts, and many courses are now available at community colleges and universities across the states. The best programs tend to be sensitive to their students and share a philosophy that carefully spells out clear principles for learning the standard.

From a perceptual view, most standard English speakers believe that black standard speakers have made a sincere attempt to improve themselves, while street speakers are often considered to be less ambitious and not as well educated; this is simply another biased view that has prevailed throughout American folk history. As is the case in every socially stratified culture, the perceptions that evolve in isolation distort the truth. Access to the standard in some form is essential for effective use. Although the above exercises could be used to learn other accents, our focus on employability views standard English as an interactional tool.

When street speakers see standard English as a tool rather than as a rejection of black culture, it will be easier to face the conflicts that bidialectal pressures can exert. The employer sees the situation in a restricted way: what is best for business? While the burden of adjustment falls squarely on minorities, this has been true throughout history—those people who have failed to adjust have often failed to survive. The diversity of black American behavior is a reflection of this adjustment, which in many cases was necessary for survival itself. Sensitive employers will be rare, even if they are sympathetic to the special culture shocks that are in store for blacks who try to compete as equals. Since this will be the case, the initial competitive edge will still belong to those who can interact with standard speakers with ease.

This fact is dramatically reinforced through the mass media, where the standards for linguistic skills are imposed by the industry. The most visible black role models, including most newscasters, typically use standard English. Street speech is often saved for less savory dramatic characters, which only reinforces the negative stereotypes that have evolved since the inception of slavery. Employers don't need to learn street speech, Spanish, or sign language in order to keep their jobs; this is simply reality. The same political fact holds for other advanced industrial societies and should therefore come as no surprise. The result of this reality, though, means that blacks who can use standard English will be perceived as being more competent than their street-speaking counterparts—even though dialect can be a misleading indicator of true talent and ability. Managers should take this into account whenever possible, because good ideas should be welcome from as many sources as possible. However, street speakers will continue to face an uphill battle, especially since growing numbers of black standard speakers are entering the job market. There are also increasing numbers of black children who learn standard English as their native dialect. Some learn street speech as a second dialect, while others never learn the vernacular. My comments are directed more at those who have learned street speech as their mother dialect, because this is still the overwhelming majority of black Americans.

Einar Haugen (1964) made a painful observation that is pertinent to the discussion at hand. He pointed out the difference between bilingualism and bidialectalism and indicated how much time and effort would be involved in teaching-learning a second dialect. He went on to inquire about the real prospects that would face these students after their linguistic toil. The reality remains the same; after all is said and done, there are no guarantees that good jobs will be waiting for black people who speak standard English. My point serves to amplify the dilemma. What few professional opportunities are available will continue to go to those who can use the standard. Furthermore, while standard English may help one get a foot in the professional door, it is not sufficient by itself to allow one to keep a job. Ultimately, skilled training of the highest caliber will continue to be the top requirement, because once blacks enter higher professional levels they will be judged by traditional competitive standards.

I will not go into full detail about the rites of passage for minorities in the professions, although some evidence exists to suggest that white women and all minorities are tested more severely during probationary periods than their white male colleagues of equal status. This is another historical reality, and the trend is likely to continue in some circles. The feeling among many is that white women and all blacks should be grateful for employment, and if they are truly good they should also be able to shoulder a larger load, especially during tight fiscal periods. It serves little purpose to condemn these attitudes, because managers will continue to do what they feel is best for business. When professional jobs are tight for white males, there are surely fewer jobs for white women and minorities. And, when choices are made between white women and minorities, a well-educated white woman will have clear cultural advantages over the streetwise competition. Familiarity with mainstream norms is an advantage that white women have over most street speakers in the same professional job market.

As long as standard English is the language of our professions, there will be strong and influential advocates for its prescriptive preservation. Blacks who can speak street speech and standard English will have two advantages. The standard will continue to be required in professional transactions, while street speech can remain as the intimate language of home and friends. With upward mobility and relocation the linguistic networks may change; the ratio of situations for street speech and standard English could invert through time. However, at this time, practicing standard English is essential to increased proficiency, and this proficiency is preferred by the overwhelming majority of professional managers who consider hiring minorities.

Each speaker must ultimately arrive at a linguistic and social solution that is most comfortable. My recognition of this rather obvious fact, regarding the linguistic demands in professional fields, is not a condemnation of street speech. Like Cockney, black street speech will survive—in one form or another—for years to come. The emphasis here is on the acquisition of new skills and does not imply the rejection or abandonment of the intimate colloquial linguistic norms that most black people find most comfortable. As such these observations are less suited to the needs of professional practitioners; rather, they are intended more for those who are interested in pragmatic aspects of traditional linguistic, social, and economic assimilation in the United States.

10

Dynamic Black Speech:
A Nonideal Linguistic State

Throughout this book I have concentrated on the street culture. This distinction becomes critical once the overall black American population is considered. Most street consultants have very few contacts with whites and have even fewer opportunities to converse with standard English speakers. There are now thousands, perhaps millions, of black Americans who likewise have limited contact with vernacular black speech. Dialect boundaries therefore don't automatically conform to racial groups. Taken collectively, black Americans speak a wide range of dialects, including impeccable standard English. The street population is a subset of black America, as illustrated in the leftmost quadrant of figure 15. The numbers refer to the combination of social domains, including living, working, and recreational situations, where blacks primarily interact with other blacks. Those who spend more time with nonblacks, in any one of these three domains, are illustrated in the three right quadrants. Those at the extreme right have the least contact with vernacular black speakers.

While street speakers comprise a significant portion of the black population, the linguistic styles that they use are just a fraction of the complete stylistic repertoire for black Americans. As expected, more frequent contact with standard speakers increases proficiency. Exposure to the media tends to increase an individual's receptive ability but seems to have little impact on speech production.

Again, the street community is not identical to the racial (black) group. Linguistic variation is common to all languages and speakers; the difference for black Americans lies in the type and range of these alternating styles and how they shift in linguistic terms. Black street speech is far more complex than most grammarians had ever imagined. As ethnographers observed so many years ago, ethnocentric research traditions tend to reinforce their myopic past. Street speech is the product of a unique linguistic history, combined with a mélange of social and evolutionary factors. Policies of rigid segregation have—quite naturally—left their mark on black American speech. To suggest that black speakers generally, or street speakers in particular, should be ashamed of their speech shows an ignorance of the facts.

Since the inception of slavery, blacks have been subjected to linguistic chauvinism. In the political context of *any* standard language, this chauvinism—this absence of linguistic tolerance—tends to be reinforced by the work of ivory-tower philosophers and grammarians who support the superiority of particular languages or dialects. This is not a new phenomenon by any means: when the Greeks pondered the great questions, they believed their language to be divine. The list of similar linguistic allegiances unfolds throughout history, especially in societies with long-standing written traditions. This work is carried on with vigor and tenacity in several well-known publications, some of them fairly recent (see Simon 1980; Newman 1974).

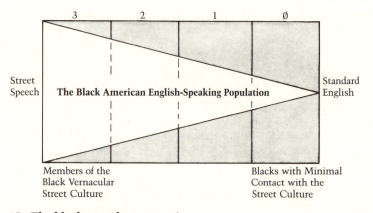

15. **The black speech community**

Through time, particularly in societies where literacy runs high, educated people have come to associate prescriptive grammar with the "best" language. This linguistic elitism has been reinforced by tradition and linguistic convention. As we observed earlier, a standard language or dialect is determined by political factors. Bonds between language and nationalism-provincialism are as old as speech itself and have spread or dwindled based on the growth and influence of the related populations. Wars, the invention of gunpowder, natural disasters, and so on are among the historical milestones that have affected the course of linguistic evolution as we know it. For several reasons, some of which are deeply personal, I have been most concerned with describing black street speech as it is used in day-to-day life. In this respect I part company with the prescriptive tradition that criticizes street speech as being linguistically deficient in contrast to the standard. Rather, descriptive linguistics has been used here as a tool, to characterize the flexible nature of street speech.

Students of linguistics and communication will appreciate the similarities which the black vernacular has with regard to other speech communities around the world, because the style shifting that we have observed with street speakers is quite common—especially among stigmatized minority (that is, less influential) groups. Beyond the linguistic realm, certain scholars like Giles and Powesland (1975) have discussed similar concepts in accommodation theory, where speakers tend to adjust their speech in the direction of other interlocutors. It therefore comes as no surprise that black America has learned to make linguistic adaptations, and in this respect we find universal linguistic implications.

When I first turned to linguistics, in the hope of learning how and why black and white dialects differ, I was naïve about the prevailing theories in the general discipline. As an outsider to the field I had assumed that at least one of the social sciences would be concerned with the objective study of language. Once exposed I soon realized, however, that few linguists had given much thought to black language, that is, prior to the civil rights movement, which triggered a flurry of research. Like other blacks of my age from the public schools, I had witnessed the double linguistic standard; I had experienced anguish and frustration when teachers would openly chastise students for their speech.

These and other pressures continue to play a role in the evolution of black dialects—today's black child will encounter a new network of speakers, as well as changing attitudes toward speech. Regardless of what is said here about street speech today, tomorrow's linguistic advances, along with the ever-changing nature of black America, will modify the dialect situation as we now see it. Having observed contemporary style shifting, we must emphasize as our main point that black speech is highly diversified and is not inferior—on linguistic grounds—to any other language or dialect. Pressures to conform to the standard will, of course, continue. We must also appreciate that these pressures are determined by political dictates and that no dialect or language is inherently superior to others in terms of logic or functional utility among native speakers. In spite of this fact, many people consider it very natural for minority groups to learn the language of the dominant group. The reverse situation, where speakers of a dominant dialect or language learn the less influential dialect or language, seems to be considered equally unnatural or uncommon at best.

Linguistics allows us to sift through this maze of emotional impressions and verbal data with greater objectivity. However, for all of the scientific merit that it affords, linguistic description alone will not be sufficient to supplant dialect attitudes that have been preserved through centuries of notorious folk etymology. The enormity of the social barriers, specifically, those maintained along dialect lines, can be addressed only one step at a time. As observed, millions of black Americans are not waiting for linguistic salvation and have adopted personal speech that serves their needs—be it standard English for television broadcasters or an eloquent vernacular for proprietors in the vernacular community. The broader problem lies not with those who are self-sufficient within the mainstream but with those who still seek participation in the face of mounting socioeconomic pressures and related hardships.

Many have pointed to the growing diversity of black America as evidence for greater minority success. This is true in terms of statistics, although vast numbers of blacks have not moved forward. In spite of the individual and group progress that has been made, more battles must be fought and won before economic rewards are distributed with greater equity among black Americans. Some are very pessimistic about the future, feeling that all the social gains from the civil rights movement will be lost without government support—which can be unpredictable. Another paradox confronts us: to paraphrase Dickens, it is the best of times, it is the worst of times. It is the best of times in the sense that more blacks than ever have attained positions of responsibility, wealth, and influence. The economic climate reflects the worst of times—black unemployment remains disproportionately high. It would be pretentious to assume that linguistic studies can reverse these social trends, but it would be more damaging to continue to believe that street speech is a simplified bastard of standard English.

I came to this study out of a combination of curiosity and life experiences from multidialectal exposure. When I became able to give this topic serious study, in 1972, I faced a different dilemma. My preliminary concerns were explicit and narrow: what is the structure of black street speech, and how did it evolve? The bidialectal situation observed thus far suggests a dynamic linguistic process for street speakers. This observation brings us back to Chomsky and to a fundamental paradox in linguistics.

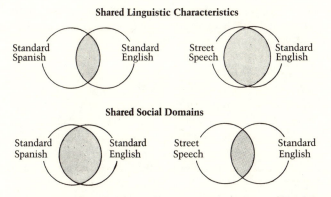

16. **Standardized bilingualism compared to nonstandard bidialectalism**

Chomsky claims that linguistics is concerned with the "ideal speaker/hearer in a homogeneous speech community" (1965 : 3). What does it mean to be an ideal street speaker? This is not a purely rhetorical question, but it is clear that a wide range of answers could apply depending on one's social relativity. Some blacks have argued that the vernacular is the language of black America (see Chennault 1981; Smitherman 1981); others have been among the most outspoken critics of the black vernacular (see Alexander 1980). Which of these positions represents the "ideal"? In spite of the hours that I spent talking to blacks about this very issue, I—perhaps more than most—am convinced that it would be extremely difficult to come to any suitable agreement regarding "ideal" black speech or the corresponding homogeneity of the community; the linguistic situation is simply too dynamic.

Haugen's distinction between a standard dialect and a nonstandard dialect serves, once again, to clarify the special linguistic problems for black America. A standard language or dialect exhibits a minimum amount of variation, both in linguistic adaptations and in socially motivated changes, yet has the broadest range of social utility. A typical standard speaker is likely to use similar styles in the living, working, and recreational domains. Nonstandard dialects, by contrast, exhibit greater linguistic variation in form and social accommodation. They are likewise restricted to a limited number of domains, say, the living and recreational settings. The bidialectal situation illustrated in figure 16 shows that functional forces, where the nonstandard vernacular operates in situations where the standard does not, are most responsible for the preservation of dialect boundaries. The shared linguistic characteristics are substantial, so much so that most Americans can carry on conversations with speakers of other regional or ethnic dialects without significant difficulty, although dialect distinctions are readily detectable.

Faced with the problem of trying to determine the "ideal" black American speaker, I had no choice but to turn to speakers in the black community for the answer. The reality there is one of diversity and change. Opinions and linguistic behavior both span broad spectra, and neither lends itself to easy delineation. To suggest anything else for black America would be false and misleading. Negative attitudes—toward racial groups or different regions of the nation—are more responsible for maintaining dialect differences than are any internal linguistic processes. Because linguistic attitudes tend to be prejudicial by nature, few people—including few linguists—are sensitive to the particular linguistic difficulties that dialect speakers encounter in the larger society.

Linguists, in the wake of the Chomskyan revolution, came to appreciate that through deductive abstraction they could travel very fast, as long as they left their social baggage at the station. Labov (1982) points to another research tradition, where social scientists conduct analyses with an eye toward public interests and welfare. The present work is cast in the latter tradition. For sociolinguistic approaches we must take care to adhere to sound principles in linguistics, since we survey the social luggage at the station, taking care to first select those bags that will enhance our descriptions.

Had I engaged in linguistic thought experiments, based on my own experiences with street speech, the subtle patterns of variation that we have observed would not have been found. The kind of variation described in chapters 5, 6, and 7 is a reflection of group behavior. Few linguists—and I include myself in this group—have the necessary background to adequately reflect on the grammaticality of black vernacular English. The most reliable consultants are those who have not been subjected to excessive exposure to the standard. As such, the study of street speech cannot be completed on university campuses alone; we must continue to have the cooperation of vernacular consultants if we are to fit together more pieces of this linguistic puzzle.

The majority of the available literature on black speech usually indicates diversity, but often only from a brief glance. There are several reasons associated with this trend, and they tend to date the corresponding works based on the prevailing social climate toward blacks when they were written. Here I have tried to step beyond the time dimension and examine aspects of street speech that are not immediately apparent to the average speaker or to the average linguist. It is my belief that sociolinguistics can serve two important functions in the short term. The most obvious contribution continues the inductive linguistic tradition; the second lies in the potential to help the consultants themselves.

All branches of science have evolved with a combination of deductive and inductive research. Linguistic deduction serves us to the extent that we can use our competence for analytic purposes. The other aspects of linguistic behavior, those which are part of our subconscious yet systematic linguistic behavior, are beyond our powers of introspection and cannot be analyzed deductively. Furthermore, in any situation where speakers have been taught that their speech is ungrammatical, we run the risk of getting biased judgments with respect to true grammatical boundaries. This is exactly the situation that faces black street speech and other nonstandard languages or dialects around the world.

In his quest for a universal linguistic theory, Chomsky dismisses the preceding reality. To claim that one can study black English—from a theoretical point of view—in the same manner that we (deductively) analyze standard dialects denies the fact that social prejudices so often influence linguistic judgments. Other language studies have echoed this fact and emphasize, once again, that all branches of science rely on a balance of inductive and deductive research. To the best of my knowledge this is true for both the physical and the social sciences.

On a more personal level the problem hits close to home, because my own linguistic experiences are too saturated with extraneous influences to insure reliable judgments. By taking the time to study street speech at first hand, as it breathes in the social milieu, we have made linguistic observations that should be of use to street speakers themselves. In this case we have exposed some dimensions of linguistic variation in street speech, as well as the historical climate that gave rise to it. And we also offer counterevidence to the racist literature on black speech.

My objective has been to use linguistic science as a tool, one that could account for distinctions between dialects. At the same time it goes without saying that dialect differences can result in social and economic hardship for millions. In much the same manner that physicists were called upon to use their expertise during World War II and geologists were faced with social problems during the eruption of Mount St. Helens, linguists can use their training—with its admitted limitations—in the search for solutions to our social problems. Having personally experienced the emotional and psychological setbacks that can result from linguistic and/or racial prejudice, I understand the frustrations that many hardworking minorities encounter when they confront dialect boundaries and uninformed criticism of their speech.

It would be just as difficult for standard speakers to master street speech as it is for black vernacular speakers to learn the standard. The social realities, however, find that standard proficiency is a more marketable skill, whereas nonstandard proficiency is still viewed as a genuine limitation. Those who choose to learn standard English will continue to make the sacrifices to do so, even if no formal training is available. Linguists now agree that languages or dialects are all equal—from a theoretical point of view. But as long as employers, educators, and politicians fail to recognize this fact, the folk notion that street speech is bad, ignorant, illogical, or inferior will prevail.

The majority of the available literature looks at black language rituals or at groups of younger speakers in very formal settings. The present study, concentrating on adult street speech and how it has evolved to accommodate several types of social situations, builds on this excellent work. These added insights into black language are intended to enrich the existing literature. Their ultimate value will come through genuine enlightenment, when—armed with further analyses—we will someday eliminate the racial barriers that have repressed valuable human resources and have kept black and other American minorities at the social, political, and economic periphery.

Bibliography

Abrahams, Roger D. 1963. *Deep down in the Jungle.* Chicago: Aldine.

——. 1976. *Talking Black.* Rowely, Mass.: Newbury House.

—— and Rudolph C. Troike. 1972. *Language and Cultural Diversity in American Education.* Englewood Cliffs, N.J.: Prentice-Hall.

Alexander, Benjamin. 1980. "Standard English, the Hell with Anything Else." In *Vital Speeches of the Day,* vol. 46, no. 14, pp. 15–21.

Bailey, Beryl. 1965. "Toward a New Perspective in Negro English Dialectology." *American Speech* 40: 171–177.

——. 1966. *Jamaican Creole Syntax.* London: Cambridge University Press.

Bailey, Charles-James N. 1973. *Variation and Linguistic Theory.* Washington, D.C.: Center for Applied Linguistics.

—— and Roger W. Shuy, eds. 1973. *Studies in New Ways of Analyzing Variation in English.* Washington, D.C.: Georgetown University Press.

Baratz, Joan C., and Roger W. Shuy. 1969. *Teaching Black Children to Read.* Washington, D.C.: Center for Applied Linguistics.

Baugh, John. 1979. "Linguistic Style Shifting in Black English." Ph.D. dissertation, University of Pennsylvania.

——. 1980. "A Reexamination of the Black English Copula." In William Labov, ed., *Locating Language in Space and Time,* pp. 83–106. New York: Academic Press.

——. 1981. "Design and Implementation of Writing Instructions for Speakers of Nonstandard English." In Bruce Cronnell, ed., *The Writing Needs of Linguistically Different Students,* pp. 17–43. Los Alamitos, Calif.: Southwest Regional Laboratory, Educational Research & Development.

Bell, J. M. 1980. *Colorphonics: An Audiovisual Vowel Identification Program for Remedial Readers.* Allen, Tex.: DLM.

Bereiter, Carl, and Siegfried Engelmann. 1966. *Teaching Disadvantaged Children in the Pre-School.* Englewood Cliffs, N.J.: Prentice-Hall.

Blom, J. P., and John J. Gumperz. 1972. "Social Meaning in Linguistic Structure: Code-Switching in Norway." In John J. Gumperz and Dell Hymes, eds., *Directions in Sociolinguistics,* pp. 207–238. New York: Holt, Rinehart & Winston.

Brown, R., and A. Gilman. 1960. "The Pronouns of Power and Solidarity." In Thomas Sebeok, ed., *Style in Language*, pp. 235–276. Cambridge, Mass.: MIT Press.

Burling, Robbins. 1973. *English in Black and White*. New York: Holt, Rinehart & Winston.

Campbell, John. 1851. *Negro Mania: An Examination of the Falsely Assumed Equality of the Various Races of Men*. Philadelphia: Campbell & Power.

Cedergren, H. C., and D. Sankoff. 1974. "Variable Rules: Performance as a Statistical Reflection of Competence." *Language* 50:333–355.

Chennault, Stephen. 1981. *Reliz Whut Ahm Talkin' 'Bout*. San Francisco: Angel Press.

Chomsky, Noam. 1957. *Syntactic Structures*. Paris: Mouton.

———. 1965. *Aspects of a Theory of Syntax*. Cambridge, Mass.: MIT Press.

———. 1977. *Language and Responsibility*. New York: Pantheon Books.

DeCamp, David, and Ian F. Hancock, eds. 1974. *Pidgins and Creoles: Current Trends and Prospects*. Washington, D.C.: Georgetown University Press.

Dillard, J. L. 1972. *Black English*. New York: Random House.

———, ed. 1975. *Perspectives on Black English*. The Hague: Mouton.

Dittmar, Norbert. 1976. *A Critical Survey of Sociolinguistics*. New York: St. Martin's Press.

Fasold, Ralph W. 1969. "Tense and the Form *Be* in Black English." *Language* 45:763–776.

———. 1972. "Decreolization and Autonomous Language Change." *Florida FL Reporter* 10: 9–12, 51.

——— and Roger W. Shuy, eds. 1970. *Teaching Standard English in the Inner City*. Washington, D.C.: Center for Applied Linguistics.

——— and ———, eds. 1975. *Analyzing Variation in Language*. Washington, D.C.: Georgetown University Press.

——— and ———, eds. 1977. *Studies in Language Variation*. Washington, D.C.: Georgetown University Press.

——— and Walter A. Wolfram. 1970. "Some Linguistic Features of Negro Dialect." In Ralph W. Fasold and Roger W. Shuy, eds., *Teaching Standard English in the Inner City*, pp. 41–86. Washington, D.C.: Center for Applied Linguistics.

Feagin, Louise Crawford. 1976. "A Sociolinguistic Study of Alabama White English." Ph.D. dissertation, Georgetown University.

———. 1979. *Variation and Change in Alabama English*. Washington, D.C.: Georgetown University Press.

Ferguson, C. A. 1959. "Diglossia." *Word* 15: 325–340.

Fickett, Joan G. 1970. *Aspects of Morphemics, Syntax, and Semiology of an Inner-City Dialect*. West Rush, N.Y.: Meadowbrook Publications.

Folb, Edith. 1980. *Runnin' down Some Lines*. Cambridge, Mass.: Harvard University Press.

Giglioli, P., ed. 1972. *Language in Social Contexts*. New York: Penguin.

Giles, Howard, and Peter Powesland. 1975. *Speech Styles and Social Evaluation.* New York: Academic Press.

Goffman, Erving. 1959. *The Presentation of Self in Everyday Life.* New York: Anchor.

———. 1963. *Behavior in Public Places.* New York: Free Press.

———. 1972. "The Neglected Situation." In P. Giglioli, ed., *Language in Social Contexts*, pp. 61–66. New York: Penguin.

Gumperz, John J., and Del Hymes, eds. 1972. *Directions in Sociolinguistics.* New York: Holt, Rinehart & Winston.

Guy, Gregory R. 1975. "Use and Application of the Cedergren-Sankoff Variable Rule Program." In Ralph W. Fasold and Roger W. Shuy, eds., *Analyzing Variation in Language*, pp. 59–69. Washington, D.C.: Georgetown University Press.

———. 1977. "A New Look at *-t, -d* Deletion." In Ralph W. Fasold and Roger W. Shuy, eds., *Studies in Language Variation*, pp. 1–11. Washington, D.C.: Georgetown University Press.

———. 1980. "Variation in the Group and the Individual: The Case of Final Stop Deletion." In William Labov, ed., *Locating Language in Space and Time*, pp. 1–36. New York: Academic Press.

Haley, Alex. 1976. *Roots.* New York: Doubleday.

Hall, Robert. 1966. *Pidgin and Creole Languages.* Ithaca: Cornell University Press.

Hall, W., and R. Freedle. 1975. *Culture and Language: The Black American Experience.* Washington, D.C.: Hemisphere Publication Co.

Hancock, Ian F. 1975. "Some Aspects of English in Liberia." In J. L. Dillard, ed., *Perspectives on Black English*, pp. 34–58. The Hague: Mouton.

Haugen, Einar. 1964. "Bilingualism and Bidialectalism." In Roger W. Shuy, ed., *Social Dialects and Language Learning*, pp. 8–9. Champaign, Ill.: National Council of Teachers of English.

———. 1972. *The Ecology of Language.* Stanford, Calif.: Stanford University Press.

Herskovits, Melville. 1941. *The Myth of the Negro Past.* New York: Harper & Brothers.

Holm, John. 1975. "Variability of the Copula in Black English and Its Creole Kin." Unpublished manuscript.

Hoover, Mary. 1975. *Appropriate Use of Black English by Black Children as Rated by Parents.* Stanford, Calif.: Stanford Center for Research and Development in Teaching.

———. 1978. "Review: Black English: A Seminar." *Journal of Psycholinguistic Research* 7: 319–325.

Hymes, Dell. 1962. "The Ethnography of Speaking." In T. Gladwin and W. C. Sturtevant, eds., *Anthropology and Human Behavior*, pp. 13–53. Washington, D.C.: Anthropological Society of Washington.

———. 1964. *Language in Culture and Society.* New York: Harper & Row.

———. 1974. *Foundations in Sociolinguistics.* Philadelphia: University of Pennsylvania Press.

————. 1978. "What Is Ethnography?" *Working Papers in Sociolinguistics* 45. Austin: Southwest Educational Development Laboratory.

Kay, Paul, and Chad McDaniel. 1979. "On the Logic of Variable Rules." *Language in Society* 8:151–188.

———— and G. Sankoff. 1974. "A Language Universals Approach to Pidgins and Creoles." In David DeCamp and Ian F. Hancock, eds., *Pidgins and Creoles: Current Trends and Prospects*, pp. 61–72. Washington, D.C.: Georgetown University Press.

Kochman, Thomas, ed. 1972. *Rappin' and Stylin' Out: Communication in Urban Black America.* Urbana: University of Illinois Press.

————. 1979. "Fighting Words: Black and White." Unpublished manuscript.

————. 1981. *Black and White Styles in Conflict.* Chicago: University of Chicago Press.

Kurath, Hans. 1949. *A Word Geography of the Eastern United States.* Ann Arbor: University of Michigan Press.

Labov, William. 1964a. "Phonological Correlates of Social Stratification." *Ethnography of Communication, American Anthropologist* 66:4–22.

————. 1964b. "Stages in the Acquisition of Standard English." In Roger W. Shuy, ed., *Social Dialects and Language Learning*, pp. 77–103. Champaign, Ill.: National Council of Teachers of English.

————. 1965. "On the Mechanism of Linguistic Change." *Georgetown Monograph Series on Languages and Linguistics* 18, pp. 27–42. Washington, D.C.: Georgetown University Press.

————. 1966. *The Social Stratification of English in New York City.* Washington, D.C.: Center for Applied Linguistics.

————. 1969. "Contraction, Deletion, and Inherent Variability of the English Copula." *Language* 45:715–762.

————. 1970a. "The Logic of Nonstandard English." In James E. Alatis, ed., *Georgetown Monograph Series on Languages and Linguistics* 22, pp. 1–44. Washington, D.C.: Georgetown University Press.

————. 1970b. *The Study of Nonstandard English.* Champaign, Ill.: National Council of Teachers of English.

————. 1971. "Methodology." In William Orr Dingwall, ed., *A Survey of Linguistic Science*, pp. 86–107. College Park: University of Maryland Linguistics Program.

————. 1972a. *Language in the Inner City: Studies in the Black English Vernacular.* Philadelphia: University of Pennsylvania Press.

————. 1972b. *Sociolinguistic Patterns.* Philadelphia: University of Pennsylvania Press.

————, ed. 1980. *Locating Language in Space and Time.* New York: Academic Press.

————. 1982. "Objectivity and Commitment in Linguistic Science: The Case of the Black English Trial in Ann Arbor." *Language in Society* 11:165–202.

————, Paul Cohen, Clarence Robins, and John Lewis. 1968. *A Study of the Non-Standard English of Negro and Puerto Rican Speakers in New York City.* USOE Final Report, Research Project 3,288.

———— and Clarence Robins. 1969. "A Note on the Relation of Reading Failure to Peer-Group Status in Urban Ghettos." In Alfred A. Aarons, Barbara Y. Gordon, and William A. Stewart, eds., *Linguistic-Cultural Differences and American Education*, Special Anthology Issue of the *Florida FL Reporter*, pp. 17–38.

Mackler, B. 1980. "Cooperation and Community: Reflection on a Model of Urban Education." *Journal of Negro Education* 49:60–66.

Milroy, Lesley. 1980. *Language and Social Networks*. Baltimore: University Park Press.

———— and James Milroy. 1976. "Speech and Context in an Urban Setting." *Belfast Working Papers in Language and Linguistics* 2.

Mitchell-Kernan, Claudia. 1969. *Language Behavior in a Black Urban Community*. Working Paper 23. Berkeley: University of California, Language-Behavior Laboratory.

Newman, Edwin. 1974. *Strictly Speaking: Will America Be the Death of English?* New York: Bobbs-Merrill.

Pfaff, Carol. 1971. "Historical and Structural Aspects of Sociolinguistic Variation: The Copula in Black English." Technical Report 37. Los Alamitos, Calif.: Southwest Regional Laboratory.

Pitts, Walter. 1981. "Beyond Hypercorrection: The Use of Emphatic /-z/ in Black English Vernacular." In *Proceedings of the 14th Meeting of the Chicago Linguistic Society*, pp. 73–87. Chicago: University of Chicago, Department of Linguistics.

Poplack, Shana. 1978a. "Dialect Acquisition among Puerto Rican Bilinguals." *Language in Society* 7:89–103.

————. 1978b. "Quantitative Analysis of Constraints on Code-Switching." City University of New York, Centro de Estudios Puertorriqueños.

Prince, Ellen. 1975. "The Nature of Aspect." Ph.D. dissertation, University of Pennsylvania.

Rickford, John R. 1974. "The Insights of the Mesolect." In David DeCamp and Ian F. Hancock, eds., *Pidgins and Creoles: Current Trends and Prospects*, pp. 92–117. Washington, D.C.: Georgetown University Press.

————. 1975. "Carrying the New Wave into Syntax: The Case of Black English *Been*." In Ralph W. Fasold and Roger W. Shuy, eds., *Analyzing Variation in Language*, pp. 162–183. Washington, D.C.: Georgetown University Press.

Roueche, Suanne. 1981. *N.I.E. Final Report on Community College Literacy*. Austin: University of Texas, College of Education.

Rousseau, Pascale, and David Sankoff. 1978. "Advances in Variable Rule Methodology." In David Sankoff, ed., *Linguistic Variation: Models and Methods*, pp. 57–70. New York: Academic Press.

Sag, Ivan. 1973. "On the State and Progress of Progressives and Statives." In Charles-James N. Bailey and Roger W. Shuy, eds., *Studies in New Ways of Analyzing Variation in English*, pp. 83–95. Washington, D.C.: Georgetown University Press.

Sankoff, David, and William Labov. 1979. "On the Uses of Variable Rules." *Language in Society* 8:189–222.

Sapir, Edward. 1912. "Language and Environment." *American Anthropologist* 14:226–242.
———. 1929. "The Status of Linguistics as a Science." *Language* 5:207–214.
———. 1931. "Dialect." *Encyclopedia of the Social Sciences* 5:123–126.
Sebeok, Thomas, ed. 1960. *Style in Language.* Cambridge, Mass.: MIT Press.
Shaw, George Bernard. 1916. *Pygmalion.* London: Cambridge University Press.
Shuy, Roger W., ed. 1964. *Social Dialects and Language Learning.* Champaign, Ill.: National Council of Teachers of English.
———, Walter A. Wolfram, and William K. Riley. 1968. *Field Techniques in an Urban Language Study.* Washington, D.C.: Center for Applied Linguistics.
Simon, John. 1980. *Paradigms Lost: Reflections on Literacy and Its Decline.* New York: Clarkson N. Potter/Crown Publishers.
Simpkins, Gary, and Grace Holt. 1977. *Bridge: A Cross-Culture Reading Program.* Boston: Houghton Mifflin Co.
Smitherman, Geneva. 1977. *Talkin' and Testifyin'.* Boston: Houghton Mifflin Co.
———, ed. 1981. *Black English and the Education of Black Children and Youth: Proceedings of the National Invitational Symposium on the King Decision.* Detroit: Wayne State University, Afro-American Studies.
Spears, Arthur. 1982. "The Black English Semi-Auxiliary *Come.*" *Language* 58:850–872.
Stack, Carol. 1974. *All Our Kin.* New York: Harper & Row.
Stewart, William A. 1967. "Sociolinguistic Factors in the History of American Negro Dialects." *Florida FL Reporter* 5:11, 22, 24, 26.
———. 1968a. "An Outline of Linguistic Typology for Describing Multilingualism." In Joshua A. Fishman, ed., *Readings in the Sociology of Language,* pp. 531–544. The Hague: Mouton.
———. 1968b. "Continuity and Change in American Negro Dialects." *Florida FL Reporter* 6:14–16, 18.
———. 1969. "The Use of Negro Dialect in the Teaching of Reading." In Joan C. Baratz and Roger W. Shuy, eds., *Teaching Black Children to Read,* pp. 159–219. Washington, D.C.: Center for Applied Linguistics.
———. 1970a. "Foreign Language Teaching Methods in Quasi–Foreign Language Situations." In Ralph W. Fasold and Roger W. Shuy, eds., *Teaching Standard English in the Inner City,* pp. 1–19. Washington, D.C.: Center for Applied Linguistics.
———. 1970b. "Toward a History of Negro Dialect." In Frederick Williams, ed., *Language and Poverty: Perspectives on a Theme,* pp. 351–379. Chicago: Markham.
Taylor, Douglas. 1977. *Languages of the West Indies.* Baltimore: Johns Hopkins University Press.
Traugott, Elizabeth C. 1972a. *A History of English Syntax.* New York: Holt, Rinehart & Winston.

————. 1972b. "Principles in the History of American English—A Reply." *Florida FL Reporter* 10: 5–6, 56.

Turner, Lorenzo. 1949. *Africanisms in the Gullah Dialect.* Chicago: University of Chicago Press.

Voorhoeve, Jan. 1962. *Sranan Syntax.* Amsterdam: North-Holland Publishing Co.

Weinreich, Uriel. 1953. *Languages in Contact.* The Hague: Mouton.

————, William Labov, and Marvin I. Herzog. 1968. "Empirical Foundations for a Theory of Language Change." In W. P. Lehmann and Yakov Malkiel, eds., *Directions for Historical Linguistics: A Symposium*, pp. 95–188. Austin: University of Texas Press.

Welmers, William E. 1973. *African Language Structures.* Berkeley and Los Angeles: University of California Press.

Williams, Frederick, ed. 1970. *Language and Poverty: Perspectives on a Theme.* Chicago: Markham.

Williamson, Juanita, and V. Burke, eds. 1976. *A Various Language.* New York: Holt, Rinehart & Winston.

Wolfram, Walter A. 1969. *A Sociolinguistic Description of Detroit Negro Speech.* Washington, D.C.: Center for Applied Linguistics.

————. 1971a. "Black-White Speech Relationships Revisited." In Walter A. Wolfram and Nona H. Clarke, eds., *Black-White Speech Relationships*, pp. 139–161. Washington, D.C.: Center for Applied Linguistics.

————. 1971b. "Sociolinguistic Alternatives for Teaching Reading to Speakers of Nonstandard English." *Reading Research Quarterly* 6: 9–33.

————. 1973a. *Sociolinguistic Aspects of Assimilation: Puerto Rican English in East Harlem.* Washington, D.C.: Center for Applied Linguistics.

————. 1973b. "On What Basis Variable Rules?" In Charles-James N. Bailey and Roger W. Shuy, eds., *Studies in New Ways of Analyzing Variation in English*, pp. 1–12. Washington, D.C.: Georgetown University Press.

————. 1974. "The Relationship of White Southern Speech to Vernacular Black English." *Language* 50: 498–527.

———— and Donna Christian. 1976. *Appalachian Speech.* Washington, D.C.: Center for Applied Linguistics.

———— and Ralph W. Fasold. 1974. *Social Dialects in American English.* Englewood Cliffs, N.J.: Prentice-Hall.

Wolfson, Nessa. 1976. "Speech Events and Natural Speech." *Language in Society* 5: 81–96.

Index